THE COMPLEXITY TRAP

WHY WE NEED A NEW MANAGEMENT APPROACH

STEPHANIE BORGERT

GABAL global
English Editions by GABAL Publishing

iUniverse®

THE COMPLEXITY TRAP
WHY WE NEED A NEW MANAGEMENT APPROACH

First published under the title "Die Irrtümer der Komplexität – Warum wir ein neues Management brauchen" in 2015 by GABAL Verlag, Germany

Illustrations Credit: Carsten Oltmann
Text Graphics Credit: Stephanie Borgert
Author Photo Credit: Jan Hillnhütter

iUniverse books may be ordered through booksellers or by contacting:

iUniverse
1663 Liberty Drive
Bloomington, IN 47403
www.iuniverse.com
1-800-Authors (1-800-288-4677)

ISBN: 978-1-5320-1952-4 (sc)
ISBN: 978-1-5320-1953-1 (e)

Library of Congress Control Number: 2017905154

Print information available on the last page.

iUniverse rev. date: 04/17/2017

"There's always something."

Contents

How to use this book

Why this book was written

I was sitting at a conference table with the marketing manager of a financial services company and one of his representatives. The three of us were there to work out the details of a coaching contract, though we were still getting warmed up. The conversation soon turned to my favorite topic: complexity. We chatted about our knowledge and experiences with regard to this issue, and the marketing manager asked me about the keys to managing successfully in complex organizations. I explained a bit, discussing concepts like non-transparency, self-organization, and simplification. The marketing manager listened for a while, and then took a deep breath. "You know, Ms. Borgert," he said, "that all sounds nice and good – but it won't really work for our company. It probably makes sense for small start-ups, but not for big corporations like ours with thousands of employees. And besides, we don't even have the right employees for it anyway."

There it is again, I thought. That strange approach to the topic of complexity: everyone is familiar with the concept, everyone experiences it, some even manage to call it by its name… and yet no one wants to do anything to deal with it. Sometimes it seems like organizations need to get turned completely inside out before becoming capable of successfully reacting to the growing complexity of our world. Concepts like "interconnectedness", "self-organization", and "unpredictability" just seem too big and mysterious for them.

Complexity (together with organizational resilience) represents the primary focus of my work as a speaker and business consultant. In recent years, I have often noticed just how little managers understand complexity. And it's not because these managers aren't smart enough – it's simply because the topic isn't even brought up in most management training programs, where the focus is still on linear methodology and causal thinking. However, this is exactly what leads to misconceptions and errors in complex contexts – and the result, on a personal level, is constant stress and overload on managers and executives.

It was right at that conference table that I decided to write this book. I wanted to take apart the most common and entrenched misconceptions that I've encountered over the years regarding the concept of complexity, and turn them into knowledge for managers. At the same time, through this book, I would like to share ideas that can provide impetus towards achieving great successes with (sometimes very) small changes. I want to demystify complexity – and to clarify what it really means for our organizations and teams, as well as how we can deal with it.

I have written this book for all managers and executives – because the topic is relevant to everyone. However, not everyone will identify with it. For this reason, I will now state clearly what this book is, to whom it is directed, and who should rather just put it aside.

What this book is

This book deals with the biggest misconceptions around the concept of complexity, in an informal yet serious manner. It explains the roots of these errors and demonstrates why people succumb to them. This is often simply a question of a person's individual mindset – of a person's own character, values, and experiences – and this book will help you get a handle on this. For every common error, there are insights that can enable us to better deal with rising complexity, and I will share these insights with you over the course of the book. Although complexity is not the cause of all errors, the effects are more substantial in complex contexts than in linear ones. Complexity is in the very nature of the subject here – so you won't find your own personal challenges directly in the examples, but rather will need to extrapolate to your own concrete contexts in order to deal with your own personal challenges. This book simply seeks to stimulate you, to encourage you to reflect, to produce those "aha" moments, to germinate new ideas in your mind, and to be fun.

What this book is not

This book is not a one-size-fits-all guide – it won't provide you any formulas or methods of the "If you do X, then Y will happen" type! Complex tasks are dynamic, non-linear, and non-transparent. It is impossible to give "best-practice solutions" for handling any complex problem, and thus you will not find any ready-made blueprints in this book. There is always the question of context – and this is a point that I will stress again and again.

How this book is organized

The book is structured in such a way that each individual chapter dealing with an individual misconception can be read on its own. In order for this to work, there is a bit of repetition between the chapters. If, while reading, you do stumble across a term that has only been defined elsewhere, then you can just take a quick look at the glossary, in which all of the most important terms are explained.

The first chapter introduces the concept of complexity and explains the key features of complex systems, such as dynamics, non-transparency, self-organization, and so on. We then move on to the nine most common complexity-related misconceptions that continue to be widespread in management circles. In the final chapter, I summarize the skills, mindsets, and competencies that are necessary for mastering complexity. By the end of the book, you will understand what it takes to be successful, in a holistic sense, as a manager and a leader – despite, or perhaps as a result of, complexity. Many of the key ideas behind holistic management are highlighted in the text.

 Key ideas are highlighted with this symbol.

For whom this book was written

I wrote this book for all managers and executives who grapple with the complexity of our world, and who want to apply the knowledge in this book towards more successful management, leadership, and decision-making. The book is aimed at people who are open to dealing with their own perspectives, stereotypes, prejudices, and clichéd narratives. If you are willing to learn new things, check them against your old habits, and, if necessary, perhaps even adapt your thinking and behavior, then I hope you gain lots of insights from reading this book.

For whom this book was not written

Anyone who is unwilling to grapple with complexity (for whatever reason) should simply put this book aside right now. You will only waste a ton of mental energy trying to rebut the information and examples given and arguing that they are impractical. If you are looking for simple formulas, you just won't find them here. So, if you are unwilling to scrutinize and reflect upon both yourself and your organization, on a fundamental level, then you need not bother reading any further.

Risks and side effects

When you delve into the topic of complexity, it is only natural to get confused from time to time. "What should I do next?" "How does that work?" "So there's no answer?" This is what happens to us when we can't see, or just can't quite grasp, a solution or answer right away. And this is actually a good thing – because it is this very state that leads to new insights, as we expand our horizons and test out different ways of thinking. So you may even want to try new things, start seeing the world differently, question things you've never questioned, and really think about yourself. And I hope that you do – and that you enjoy yourself in the process!

**Complexity:
Myth or Reality?**

Many symptoms – with one diagnosis

"Everything's gone haywire."
"We're sinking into chaos."
"There's just not enough data."
"We've got to get a grip on things."
"This is just too complex – we need to simplify it."
"Everyone just does whatever they want here."
"How are we supposed to plan this?"
"We need more information to make a decision."
"This has just gotten too big for us."

How many of these lines have you either spoken yourself or heard from colleagues, superiors, or employees recently? It is quite likely that you have encountered more than one of them. I hear such statements often in the course of my work with executives and project teams – and the list could be expanded quite easily, as there are countless different ways to describe "chaos" (➡ Glossary). We always use this term when a situation seems to have gotten out of control and when we've lost the big picture. It also makes clear that the circumstances themselves have made matters difficult for us – not our own lack of competence or anything of the sort.

Many of these lines have become almost like mantras that get repeated constantly throughout organizations, while we search for an explanation for the ever-increasing chaos. Didn't everything used to be much simpler and easier? Now, stress levels are on the rise, everything's become more dynamic, each new change leads to yet another change, and no one can wrap their head around things anymore.

Fortunately, for some years now, we have had a valid explanation for the chaos: complexity. Countless articles, books, and papers have been written about this (supposedly) modern societal symptom. Studies cite project managers declaring that complexity is one of the greatest problems faced in management nowadays. Managers are asked to what extent complexity is a challenge for them. The analyses reflect upon how complexity can be eliminated, or at least gotten under control. Complexity is a cause, symptom, problem, challenge, and demon – all at the same time.

We have found our explanation – we now know why we regularly find ourselves stuck in chaos. The concept of complexity is recent; the term gets used often and indiscriminately. However, the many publications on the topic only rarely address what exactly complexity means, what it represents, and how we can deal with it.

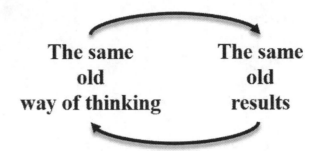

When things change, our mental model needs to change too.

The complexity of the (working) world, as we have created it, is neither a problem itself nor the cause of any problem. It is not something that we can eliminate or reduce. It will never disappear completely. Our world is complex and will remain complex – and we need to get used to this and accept it. Complexity is not our enemy. It is merely the state of affairs in which we all live and operate. There is no question of reducing complexity; rather, the question is being able to deal with it. How can we successfully operate in a complex environment?

Numerous different responses are given to this question – such as "There's nothing we can do, the system just is what it is" or "We need to develop some sort of method". Passing responsibility off to "the system" seems simple and promising, but is basically tantamount to playing dead in the face of a saber-toothed tiger. Wanting to search for methods likewise stems from our desire for security and simplicity. We are already familiar with these two approaches – so we simply resort to what is known when we are faced with new, unknown challenges. And this is just the point: complexity is the great unknown when it comes to the management of modern organizations. We still don't understand it well enough and we have no idea what tools we can use to deal with it.

In my consulting work, I am constantly confronted with misconceptions and fallacies in connection with the concept of complexity. This is mostly due to managers' lack of information and reflection with regard to their own contexts, rather than a lack of managerial competence on their part. Additionally, people always tend to isolate some root cause behind any problem or behavior, thinking that this means they can understand it. We phrase our statements like "X, therefore Y" – certain that we can find a causal connection for every situation. And this brings us to the first of several management dogmas that we work with in our consulting sessions.

"There's always a cause and effect." All throughout our education, we are trained to think in terms of cause-and-effect relationships. This leads to statements like, "We won't reach the project goals because the department of X didn't buy into the plan" or "Steve Jobs is the reason for Apple's success". Very simple: there is a cause and an effect. We find tons of explanations of this sort when we look back at past events, whether successes or failures – someone always says "I knew it!" And even looking forward to the future, people "know" exactly what needs to be done in order to reach a goal, making statements like "If we manage to get the right message across on the website, then the marketing will take care of itself" or "If we want to strengthen the team, then we'll need to organize a team-building event".

But neither a project, nor a company like Apple, nor a team constitutes a simple system that can be characterized linearly. On the contrary, such entities are quite complex – and cannot be broken down into simple cause-and-effect chains, at least not a priori. Causality is often confused with correlation in this regard. A complex system (➡ Glossary) consists of interrelationships between its component parts. In order to understand the system, we need to focus on these relationships and their reciprocal interactions.

"It just can't work with so many people involved." When it comes to complex projects, this is one of the most common ways that people rationalize failure. With too many participants in a project – so the thinking goes – it gets too complex, which leads to "nothing actually getting done". This, however, is a fallacy. Having lots of participants does not necessarily bring about complexity. When an army is marching in step, there are lots of soldiers participating – yet it remains linear. Complexity comes about as a result of interconnectedness (➡ Glossary) between participants. This brings about reciprocal interactions and dynamics, rattling our cause-and-effect thinking. We will examine this point in more detail when discussing other misconceptions, but for now it will suffice to note the following: The problem arises when we try to manage a large, *complex* system in the exact same way as we would manage a large, *linear* system.

"We need to ensure stability." I don't know of any organization that is not in a constant state of change. There are always several ongoing projects and processes running in parallel to enable the organization to respond to changing conditions. Nevertheless, the idea has taken hold in the minds of many executives that one of their key goals must be stability – almost as a counter-pole to change. Even if we were to be able to achieve true stability, there would eventually be no new ideas, no innovation, and no new solutions. A complex system that remains stable in the long term will end up paying a price in terms of flexibility. We need to accept this – and learn how to deal with constant change. This is true on the employee level as well. Managers must also ensure moments of respite, of course – but this has nothing to do with the stability of the system itself.

"We have to be on the same page." Many managers stick to the idea that solving complex tasks requires complete harmony and one-hundred-percent agreement between team members – thinking that only when everyone shares the same point of view are they ready to tackle difficult problems. This misconception probably arises from the diffuse notion that complexity and "following orders" don't go well together. However, complex tasks and contexts necessitate just the *opposite* of complete conformity among participants. They require discourse, in the truest sense of the word. It is essential that there be genuine debate, bringing together diverse perspectives, opinions, and skills. Complexity requires diversity on every level.

"Self-organization is when everything runs on its own." "Does your team work in a self-organized manner?" "Yes, it's great – I barely have to do anything at all." Do you think I just made up this exchange? Unfortunately, no. There are as many misconceptions surrounding the concept of "self-organization" as there are regarding complexity itself. Self-organization implies the opposite of "I don't have to do anything". *Every* complex system is self-organized – you can influence it, disturb it, or try to impede it, but it remains self-organized. If you "do nothing" as a manager and still come out with the right results at the end, then congratulations – either you got lucky or someone else took the lead. Discipline, rules, and feedback form the basis of successful self-organization. Only a system that constantly checks its direction and responds to feedback has a chance to aim for its goals, without relying on luck.

There are countless definitions, explanations, and misconceptions surrounding the concept of complexity. Thus, what immediately follows is a closer examination of this concept, as well as the key features of complex systems. Then, on the basis of this foundational understanding, we will move on to sketching out and resolving the most common misconceptions about complexity. In the process, we will examine both the individual level (on which the misconception arises) as well as the system level (on which it usually manifests itself).

Complexity in a nutshell

Is complexity really a new phenomenon? No. Then why must it suddenly be dealt with now? Because the level of complexity within organizations nowadays is increasingly revealing the limits of our decision-making and leadership capabilities. Complex systems are no trendy development – however, as a management issue, they have become significantly more relevant in recent decades.

This is largely a result of increased interconnectedness. The degree of complexity in society as a whole has exploded – but especially in the working world. The internet, new media, and globalization are just a few of the main buzzwords here. Unlike earlier, we now deal with systems that are composed of many components (or participants), which, in turn, are highly interconnected. This interconnectedness involves internal dynamics, non-linear relationships (➡ Glossary) and non-transparency.

Systems theories have been telling us this for decades, but they have been largely ignored in management circles. For a long time, the prevailing view was that "complex" was merely another word for "complicated" (➡ Glossary), and that one just needed to choose the right analyses and methods in order to be successful. The first step in leaving this school of thought behind is recognizing and accepting the complexity of one's organization, project, problem, or task – the system.

Organizations, projects, etc. are complex because:

➤ they are open, with regard to the exchange of information (➡ Glossary), resources, etc., with their environment.
➤ there are many participants acting independently of one another, each one on the basis of heuristics (➡ Glossary) and local information.
➤ non-linear internal dynamics ensure that there are "surprises".
➤ they are constantly changing.
➤ their behavior is unpredictable.

If you can check off these five points, that is a good indication that your system is complex. There are no longer any clear or optimal solution spaces, and many structures or processes manifest themselves only indirectly. And this is exactly where we are faced with our current management challenges, as it means that decisions must be made with less certainty. It means that decisions must be made with limited resources (i.e., information, time, material, knowledge) at hand. Many people feel overwhelmed by this, especially in turbulent or critical situations.

All of this, of course, still tells you nothing about *how* to successfully manage and lead in complex systems. There are also several fundamental aspects of complexity that should be clearly understood in order to avoid succumbing to any misconceptions – and falling into the complexity trap. The key features of complex systems, along with their effects, are defined below on the basis of systems theory, in order to enable you to better understand such matters. These concepts will also be referenced throughout later chapters, although they will not be explained anew each time – a quick glance in the glossary at the end of the book may be useful at such points.

The aspects of complex systems

Complexity (➡ Glossary): For the purposes of this book, we use a definition of complexity that relates to the number of factors (parts or parties involved) and their reciprocal relationships. The degree of complexity is a product of these two variables. The more parties involved and the more interconnected they are, the greater the degree of complexity in the system. Once a system reaches a certain degree of complexity, it can no longer be fully grasped or taken stock of cognitively.

Interdependence (➡ Glossary): What happens if particular parts of the system are removed? How big is the effect? Are those parts system-relevant? These questions are the first steps towards understanding interconnectedness and reciprocal interactions.

Dynamics (➡ Glossary): As a result of interconnectedness, there are always reciprocal interactions in a complex system. This leads to an increased rate of change. A dynamic system does not wait for decisions or anything else – it evolves constantly, which results in a certain time pressure for management. Additionally, one cannot just observe the status quo of such a system when making decisions – one must consider the future and all courses of action associated with it. Otherwise, one will end up making decisions on the basis of a too-simplistic view of the situation.

Non-transparency (➡ Glossary): A complex system cannot be grasped fully; it must always be worked on via a partial image or cross-section. In doing so, the rest of the system and its interactions remain obscured and unknown. This inherent characteristic of complex systems results in uncertainty in planning and decision-making – yet one has no choice but to accept it.

Feedback (➡ Glossary): Feedback is the central regulation mechanism in complex systems. Information flows into the system, and has either a reinforcing or inhibitory effect. Positive feedback reinforces, while negative feedback inhibits. Most managers are hardly aware of this mechanism of complex systems, and thus do not take advantage of it sufficiently.

Self-organization (➡ Glossary): The interactions between participants in a system give rise to a certain order (as well as a tendency to maintain it), which is dependent upon the dynamics of the system. The order (➡ Glossary) that develops can only be understood if one understands the reciprocal interactions within the system. External influences can never fully explain how the order emerges within the system. Why a market is rising or falling, for example, can only be explained adequately if one considers all of the interactions within the market. A system is not organized from the outside – neither by management nor by any other external force. Self-organization is inherent in a system; it is facilitated by constraints (rules) and dynamics. Many managers think that one of their responsibilities is to "make" self-organization happen – while, in reality, they merely need to stop impeding the process.

Stability (➡ Glossary): A system that weathers slight volatility, or that quickly recovers its original state after periods of volatility, is called "stable". The more successful a system is in this regard, the more robust it is. In a changing environment, robustness is not necessarily the most highly desirable condition, as it leads to inflexibility. Thus, in this book, we are speaking of "dynamic stability". This means that a system maintains its integrity even in the event of disturbances. It can, however, modify or regenerate itself in the process.

Constraints (➡ Glossary): Even complex systems operate within their own framework and are subject to constraints. These affect the system, and are affected by the system as well. The unwritten rules within an organization, for example, serve as constraints – each and every employee quickly learns what is okay and what is not okay within the organization and within the team. The behavior of the individual employees, in turn, influences the constraints themselves and can modify or rescind them.

Variety (➡ Glossary): Variety exists through the full repertory of behavioral, communication, and decision-making possibilities within a system. This determines the amount of different possible states that a system may take on. Cybernetics pioneer William Ross Ashby formulated a "Law of Requisite Variety"

("Ashby's Law"), which states that in order to control a complex system, one must manifest at least as much variety as the system itself. Complex systems require complex responses – and organizations must be complex themselves if they are to be viable and successful in a complex environment. If a complex task is handled by an individual manager, instead of the relevant team, then the problem to be solved will be countered by the complexity of that manager alone.

When we become aware of these features of complex systems and view them in the context of concrete situations and organizations, it quickly becomes clear why we sometimes think we are sinking into chaos. It is difficult to accept that we cannot fully get a handle on complex challenges. Yet we often try to do so anyway, gathering tons of data and carrying out countless analyses – always looking for a complete picture that will yield clear decisions.

Complex systems are also characterized by their interrelationships. This makes them unpredictable; we cannot foresee how they will behave. A small change can have a large effect – the so-called "butterfly effect". But in management, the expectation of predictability can be seen everywhere – in all the forecasts, projections, objectives, and project plans. As these two worlds clash, so many managers run into a dilemma.

It is also impossible to know the solution for a complex problem in advance – in fact, it may be that no "optimal" solution even exists. Different possible solutions may be in direct competition with each other. This makes decision-making even more difficult. Complexity means constant change. Basic conditions undergo changes as a result of internal dynamics – and, in order to persevere, one must constantly be flexible in adapting to these changes, in planning under uncertain conditions, and in making one's decisions.

> *"It is not because things are difficult that we do not dare, it is because we do not dare that they are difficult."*
> LUCIUS ANNAEUS SENECA

From your own experience, you probably know well enough what complex systems look like in practice within organizations. Still, I would like to sketch out an example of one such system, as it demonstrates quite clearly the pitfalls that complexity holds for managers.

Drought, corn, money, and aid – a complex system

In May 2002, the World Food Programme (WFP) declared Zambia and five of its southern African neighbors to be disaster areas, as a result of the prolonged drought in the region. The machinery of international food aid was set in motion, making sure that more than 1,000 tons of food got delivered to Zambia within a short period of time. The aid came exclusively from non-African nations – the lion's share in the form of corn from the U.S.A. The media picked up on the (impending) famine and asked for generous donations around the world – otherwise, they predicted, hundreds of thousands of people would die by the end of the year.

But what had really happened here? In the spring of 2002, Zambia had requested a minimal amount of aid to get them through to the next harvest. Only one of its nine provinces was affected by the ongoing drought. According to the government, they still had supplies of corn from their own farmers. The shortage was local and temporary, and there was no serious famine of any sort. It is unclear whether no one heard these things or no one wanted to hear them – but, in any case, the WFP made sure that ton after ton of corn from the U.S.A. was delivered to Zambia. It is important to note that the corn in question here was transgenic, i.e., genetically modified.

In September 2002, Zambia's president, Levy Mwanawasa, took the stand at the World Summit in Johannesburg and announced that his country would not be accepting the shipments of corn from the U.S.A. He asked for no further transgenic corn to be sent to Zambia, due to worries about the effects of consuming and cultivating such corn. Twenty-seven thousand tons of corn were transported from Zambia to Malawi and distributed there. The request that no more genetically modified corn be delivered to Zambia sparked indignation on the part of the Americans. The responsible parties argued that such corn was the way forward technologically – and that the American people themselves eat it too.

In 2002, the U.S.A. supplied about 80 percent of the food aid that was delivered to southern Africa through the WFP. It is the world's number one food supplier in regions affected by crisis and famine. This started after the Second World War, when the country provided Europe with food assistance under the Marshall Plan. In the 1950's, after European agriculture was up and running again, American farmers were still producing enormous surpluses and asked the country's government to help them sell these goods. In 1954, the Agricultural Trade Development and Assistance Act (PL-480) was passed. This law set forth the framework for managing the U.S.A.'s agricultural surplus and humanitarian aid around the world. Among other provisions, it stipulated that the country should only export and use American products as food aid.

The agency responsible for coordinating this aid is named USAID (United States Agency for International Development). It may only export products from American farmers, shipped in packaging from American manufacturers, imprinted by American printing companies, and transported via American logistics companies. The legislation thus does not provide for any monetary donations to other countries, as these would do nothing to foster the nation's own economy. By its own account, one of USAID's greatest challenges is predicting when, where, and how much food will be needed around the world. Ultimately, around one million Americans are dependent on the food aid "sector".

The European Union has been providing aid to disaster areas since 1997, largely in the form of monetary donations. Delivery of seeds and food is not fundamentally barred under European law, but is no longer practiced for the most part. The reasoning is that monetary donations better enable disaster areas to resolve their own problems, rather than merely alleviating acute symptoms.

There are medium- and long-term effects when disaster areas – whether in Zambia or elsewhere – receive direct deliveries of food aid. These deliveries tend to go to urban centers, while rural areas are hardly reached at all. This leads to more urbanization in the long term, as people leave their villages to settle where there is food to be found, thus affecting the country's infrastructure. Food assistance also has a direct effect on local prices. It makes it more difficult for farmers to sell their own products. And the aid deliveries do not always contains foods that are typical to the country receiving them – thus sometimes affecting the consumption patterns of the local people as well.

In 2002, the debate heated up around genetically modified corn. Zambia accused the U.S.A. of only pursuing its own interests with regard to its technologies, without any consideration for the nations receiving the aid. According to the Zambia's president, there could be uncontrolled modifications in the seeds over time. Corn is also a staple food in Africa, and the effects of human consumption of transgenic corn were still not entirely known, he said. There was just too much uncertainty for him.

The U.S.A. replied that Zambia could resolve all its worries about the seeds by milling or boiling the corn. They also accused Zambia of rejecting the delivery of transgenic corn "all of a sudden" – after the country had been readily accepting such deliveries from the U.S.A. for decades. The U.S.A. suspected that the change may have been due to the influence of the European Union, which the U.S.A. likewise accused of pursuing its own purely economic interests and political intrigue. The E.U., for its part, accused the U.S.A. of running its foreign aid program on the basis of profit maximization. Are you still following?

All three parties to the tussle were in agreement that there were conflicts on various levels – international food aid, genetically modified corn, economics, and politics. Enoch Kavindele, Zambia's vice president, summed up the situation during an interview – noting that the Zambia's 2002 crisis showed that the E.U. and the U.S.A. were fighting their own battle on the back of southern Africa. "When two elephants fight," he said, "it is the grass that suffers."

Granted, this is only a very small fragment of the "international food aid" system – but it suffices to clearly demonstrate the key features of complex systems. In this example, we can recognize dynamics that are found in many other organizations as well – they merely relate to different topics, roles, problems, and parties. I would now like to highlight and take a closer look at some of the key facets of complexity in the context of this example. This is a topic into which morality can creep quite quickly – but I will intentionally ignore this aspect in the following analysis.

Multitude of factors: Zambia, a country with nine provinces (at the time), itself already constitutes a system with millions of people, its own laws, various internal and external influences, events such as droughts, and so on. Looking at the "international food aid" system now, we must include all of the other nations that participate in this system – along with their commodities, their people, their internal and external interrelationships, etc. This system, on the basis of its complexity alone, is far beyond easy comprehensibility. The large numbers of different factors and interrelationships render the international food aid system highly complex. Even without drawing up the boundaries of the system, you can imagine that there are numerous other "external" factors that influence it – commodities exchanges, for example, where financial wagers on agricultural resources influence prices, which in turn end up affecting food assistance programs and individual nations. On the basis of their own local influences, the parties act largely independently of each other.

Unpredictability (➡ Glossary): The international food aid system's non-linearity makes it impossible to predict. Small changes, affecting a single element of the system, can produce large effects. Let's look at Zambia's shocking rejection of the U.S.A.'s delivery of transgenic corn and its demand that only "normal" corn be delivered in the future – this change was unpredictable, and it was not a small change. There may have been weak signals that Zambia's government would be taking a stand against genetically modified food; however, these signals had brought about no resonance in the system.

Constraints: The agency that administers aid on behalf of the U.S.A. (USAID) is only allowed to purchase American commodities – it cannot distribute cash donations to famine-stricken regions. Additionally, when it comes to packaging, stickers, palettes, etc., it is obligated to choose only domestic manufacturers and products. These constraints have created a large market in the U.S.A. that is highly dependent upon foreign humanitarian aid. In other words, the system of the U.S.A. has changed itself through this constraint.

When receiving only deliveries of food aid, assistance-receiving nations have less opportunity to solve their problems than when receiving equipment, know-how, and money. This constraint contributes to the aforementioned problems such as urbanization and price declines. When a complex system changes as a result of its constraints, this also has a reactive effect on the constraints themselves. This can be seen in the expansion of aid payments from the E.U. since 1997 – the constraint has been relaxed and assistance has been increasingly administered in the form of monetary donations.

Control: The food aid example clearly demonstrates that, in a complex system, it just doesn't work to have matters predetermined by a central control. In this example, the WFP decides which countries will be declared disaster areas and then starts the flow of food deliveries. This hardly made any sense for Zambia in 2002, as the country only needed minimal short-term assistance. The feedback that Zambia's government attempted to provide was not heard, or at least was not listened to. Rather, the entire system seemed to suffer under attempts at centralized control. The U.S.A. attempted to exercise control in terms of its export-related economic interests, while the WFP continued to control the quantities and times of the aid deliveries. The parties were trying to influence the food assistance system through control, rather than working *within* the system. This can work with regard to individual short-term goals, but quickly starts manifesting inhibitive effects on the macro level.

Stability: Any presumption that the supply of commodities should ensure stability is as naïve as its opposite would be. In an acute, short-term crisis, where there is a risk of people starving, the provision of commodities indeed does help bring about a re-stabilization. The time horizon is key here, as stabilizing measures are necessary if a system becomes chaotic. This is why Zambia requested assistance to take it through to the next harvest. The country had long had experience with "stabilizing measures" and had noted with concern the changes to its own infrastructure. What stabilizes during chaotic phases quickly leads to simplification. Receiving quick supplies of food (instead of stimulating one's own agricultural production) does not lead to lasting stability.

Scaling (➡ Glossary): Food aid is a complex, dynamic system. It contains many sub-systems, with a great variety of boundaries separating each one from neighboring systems. The U.S.A., for example, sees itself as a system in itself and, at the same time, as an element of the WFP system. It draws a clear boundary between itself and Europe and Africa, while simultaneously remaining open with regard to intercommunication. The E.U. is sub-system as well, as is Zambia. The question thus arises of how exactly we are to define the "international food aid" system. The definition of the system depends on its boundaries. What constitutes part of the system, and what does not? On the micro level, we can also consider the individual farmers, people, resources, and so on. Scaling, or selecting which different levels to observe, is essential when analyzing a complex system. The diverse levels reveal diverse patterns, effects, symptoms, and problems. In order to understand interrelationships in complex systems, various levels must be considered simultaneously.

System dynamics (➡ Glossary): While reading these last few pages, you may have been thinking that international food aid is all about self-interest, politics, and chasing one's own goals. And I agree – that is what it's always about. In this system as well, there are overarching goals, covert goals, non-goals, and conflicting goals. It is often no different in our own projects and organizations – and this is what brings about system dynamics.

Sticking to the international food aid example: The U.S.A. (vociferously) urges more emergency aid, with the aim of fostering this market and generating more revenue. There is no question that they do want to offer humanitarian assistance as well. The E.U. (also vociferously) frames their primary goal as the elimination of famine. The two goals, at first glance, do not need to be mutually exclusive – however, past experience has shown that they give rise to dynamics that lead to conflict, instead of cooperation.

Goals also result in decisions and actions that affect the system. It makes a difference whether corn or cash is delivered. Each decision or action also has effects and side effects, which may only become apparent indirectly or over the long term – but which affect the system as well. It's not about smoothing everything out – it's about discovering and understanding the dynamics of the complex system. If one does so, then one can impact the system. If not, then the system merely "happens".

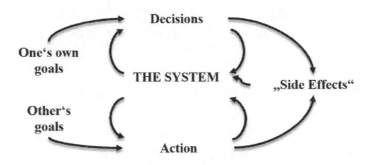

No man is an island.

It is quite easy for anyone to come up with diagnoses of what is wrong with the international food aid system. One can invoke the parties' self-interest, certain countries' inability to stimulate agricultural production, individual donor nations' arrogance, climate change, etcetera, etcetera, etcetera. People often treat such diagnoses as absolute truths – forgetting that they are only looking at a snapshot, and only from purely causal perspective. Besides such things as self-interest and conflicting goals, it is specifically our own actions that often clash with the nature of complex systems. We try to control things right down to the last detail, presuming that we understand all the causes and effects. These basic presumptions lie at the root of most errors made with regard to complexity. We need to understand complexity itself if we are to avoid the most common mistakes made in dealing with complex systems.

"A boat doesn't go forward if each one is rowing their own way."
SWAHILI PROVERB

Complexity – it's all in how you manage it

In the chapters that follow, individual misunderstandings related to complexity will be explained in great detail. When these misunderstandings go unrecognized, they lead to problems and bad decisions. There are even some fundamental mistakes that we make after having long understood and accepted complexity. This especially happens when we are thrust into an unfamiliar, tumultuous, or stressful situation. Why? Do managers and executives lack skills, or are they even simply ignorant? Are they reluctant or unable to adapt to a changing world? Well, it's a little bit of everything, and it happens without any ill intentions at all.

Our brains' CPU and memory are both limited, so we must utilize them as economically as possible. This leads us to try to reduce the complexity of the challenges that we face – so we trace events back to specific causes, enabling us to make quick and easy decisions, and we evaluate current situations on the basis of our past experiences, always making our decisions based on what is known to us. Our brain uses a "first-fit" algorithm, rather than a "best-fit" method – in other words, it takes the first acceptable solution, rather than continuing to search until it finds the best one. This economical strategy affects our thinking and behavior, and is something of which we should be aware.

"Two dangers constantly threaten the world: order and disorder."
PAUL VALÉRY

How we perceive and recall the world is always different from the world itself. We filter, omit, and distort things to create our own mental model. There is a gap between our model and the reality, which becomes especially apparent when our methods and techniques stop working. We then try to reduce this gap, either by adapting our model to fit the world or by adapting the world to fit our model.

In order to bring our own mental models up to date, it is sometimes necessary for us to admit mistakes, learn new things, or change our opinions – but such behaviors are often avoided, as they can be construed as resulting from a lack of competence. Instead, it seems easier to try to fit the world to our models, framing the truth as we see it and establishing dogmas. "That's the way we've always done it, and it's served us well." "There's obviously there's no other option – end of discussion." Complexity, though, does require us to constantly check and update our mental models.

Working and managing in complex systems, we constantly must deal with non-transparency, unpredictability, and surprises. Doing so takes many people to the limits of their competencies. Competency forms the basis for organizing one's actions, and those who are not confident in their own abilities are either slow or simply unable to act. They rather concern themselves with preserving their own self-confidence, which quickly leads to a distorted perception of the world. Some go so far as to turn a blind eye to their own failures and block out incompatible information – or even blame others' incompetency for their own problems.

There are several symptoms that are indicative of an unsuitable approach to handling complexity. I set forth the most common of these below, so that you can check whether they are present within your organization.

Indications that complexity is being handled incorrectly:

➢ Fighting symptoms instead of causes: Only what is seen gets fixed, but no one actually looks into what is actually causing the symptom – rather, the symptom itself is simply treated as the problem.

➢ Overgeneralization: A few (often unrelated) events lead to general rules and conclusions for both similar and dissimilar situations in the future.

➢ Blind faith in methods: New methods are constantly developed, or existing methods revised, with the goal of avoiding future errors and rendering uncertainties more "certain" – and the roots of problems are almost invariably sought through these methods.

➢ Excess projects: "If you don't know what else to do, create a working group." As soon as there's no easy solution to a problem, a new project is initiated to handle it. Whenever there is a huge number of project groups, their actual usefulness is suspect.

➢ The mad rush: Many people jump into tasks right away, without bothering to plan things out first. And it is precisely when a task seems intractable and they lack the big picture that they get especially busy with tons of "work".

➢ Short-term thinking: Decisions are made taking into account only their direct effects in the near future, rather than considering longer-term effects. Time-frames are usually defined by parameters (e.g., project duration, contract term, board of directors appointments) that have nothing to do with the system itself.

➢ Defending mental models at all costs: "My way of thinking is right!"

➢ Feedback neither heard nor understood: The complex system's regulation mechanism is ignored – and no critiques, affirmations, ideas, suggestions, or weak signals find their way back into the system.

➢ Lack of "system thinking": Linear, cause-and-effect relationships form the basis of thinking, discussion, and planning – while complex interrelationships are not taken into account. The focus remains on individual details, while the big picture is ignored.

That, dear reader, is the context in which you operate. Can it ever be simple to successfully manage an organization under these conditions? No. But are there approaches, ideas, and tools that can be useful for mastering complexity? Yes. Can it be enjoyable? Absolutely. And will this book help? Definitely – enabling you to clear up misconceptions and expand your own mental model.

SUMMING UP:

- ❖ Our world is complex. This is not a problem – it's just a condition that we must deal with.
- ❖ Complexity creates an unclear picture.
- ❖ Complex systems are interconnected, dynamic, non-transparent, and unpredictable.
- ❖ Complex problems require complex answers – not simple ones.
- ❖ Our mental models need to be brought up to date.

Misconception #1:
Simplicity leads to success

"It could all be so simple, but it's not..." – the German band Die Fantastischen Vier hit the nail on the head with this lyric. This is exactly what everyone has been preaching to us. But when did we develop this obsession with simplicity? Was it in the late 70s, when Canon began touting their newest camera as being "so advanced, it's simple"? Or maybe in 2002, when John Maeda published his bestseller *The Laws of Simplicity*? By now, everywhere we go, people are trying to sell us on what's "simple".

Commercials on TV show us just how simple (➡ Glossary) everything can be. If your wineglasses are clean, then you'll get along great with your neighbors – there's a clear cause and a clear effect. It's simple! And just take a look around your local bookstore – you'll find books ranging from *Dinner Made Simple* to *Taxes Made Simple* to *Spanish Made Simple*.

My personal favorite is the *Simplify...* series of books. Starting with *Simplify your life*, it turned into a collection of ideas for people to simplify all sorts of different aspects of their lives – from *Simplify your love* to *Simplify your time* to *Simplify your day* and so on. Everything's so simple! What I like most about this series is its practicality, coupled with the well-founded concept behind it: that the mere act of cleaning up helps make a person happier. Yes, it's that simple – you probably never would have imagined it, but the idea is that cleaning pushes people into action, making them no longer merely reactive. And this automatically makes them happy. It's great, and it's so simple.

We are living in an age in which everything is more dynamic – a highly complex age, marked by rapid change and extreme interconnectedness. So how can we harmonize this with the "simplicity principle"? All the gurus and article writers have their answer to this question too – in the form of checklists. And they grab your attention too, with titles like "The five most common management mistakes" or "11 tips for avoiding burn-out" or "7 tips for effective project communication" or "The 4 worst e-mail sins". From A to Z, the internet is full of listicles and advice for you to apply in your everyday life.

And if all the books and advice articles aren't enough for you, then you might end up attending one of the ballyhooed seminars on the topic of simplicity. Perhaps one called "Reduce complexity", full of best-practice examples from the real world. Best practice is to complexity as Six Sigma is to innovation – the formulas that these seminars share will never actually make you more successful because they are not adjusted to your own individual context. There will, however, be lots of strategies, tools, and techniques that can contribute to increased efficiency and effectiveness, despite or even owing to the increased complexity. At the end of the day, it will probably amount to nothing more than a general personal and time management seminar – which you could have just sought out directly under this description instead.

Of course, the consultants have also picked up on this simplification trend and postulated entire plans for "mastering complexity". It's especially great when they present you with a 5-point plan as a checklist to follow. These plans are very simple – because there's simply nothing new about them, and they have nothing at all to do with complexity. Why does all of this exist? Why do we love working with these checklists? Why do we want everything to be simple?

Simplicity gives us certainty and a sense of direction. No confusion, no headwind – we can feel our way forward. Simplification leads us to believe that there is always a clear cause-and-effect relationship. This helps orient us – we know what needs to be done. Very simple.

Just so that you don't get the wrong impression here, I will note that some of these books and plans do contain good ideas. It's just that sometimes they are called "simple" when they really are anything but. Many promise things that simply cannot be promised. Enough with this! How can a person develop a "healthy" attitude towards complexity if they're always being promised that they can just get rid of it? Maybe let's take another look at the lyrics of Die Fantastischen Vier's song:

"Close your eyes and take a deep breath and stop just believing in what you see. You know quite well that figuring everything out is something that you will never manage to do. So what you need is trust and imagination. There's one way in which we're all the same, even if it doesn't seem that way to anyone. We know nothing, but everyone else knows – and in this, we are all united."

Simplicity offers certainty

If someone wants to request vacation time at your company, what is the procedure like? It's probably quite clear. Regardless of whether the process is automated or manual, you will need to specify the time period of your vacation and submit an appropriate request to your supervisor for approval. Your supervisor will then give his approval and forward it to the HR department. The process probably works something like that. It was explained to you when you joined the company, and you followed it the first time you took time off. It was simple. From then on, whenever you want to request time off from work, you don't need to think too much about the procedure – you know that it will be the same. This gives you a sense of certainty.

Whether it's a vacation time request or anything else in life, we like having certainty. We like knowing what to do – and knowing what result to expect from it. The need for certainty is deeply ingrained in mankind, and we crave it for evolutionary reasons. In ancient times, fear was an essential tool that protected us from risks; it still has a life-preserving function to this day, even if we do sometimes need to distinguish between "real" risks and "subjective" fears. Ultimately, of course, fear is always subjective, and thus always genuine – even when you are not confronted with any "objective" risk. Fear ensures that we escape from risks, rather than expose ourselves to them. Although matters of life and death are rather less common in our modern working world, this mechanism continues to survive inside us – along with the accompanying latent aversion to uncertainty and not knowing.

Our ancestors had no time to ponder what to do when standing face-to-face with a saber-toothed tiger – they had to react immediately. Although the complex problems in our working lives are generally not life-threatening, they still inherently put us under time pressure. Circumstances demand quick solutions, often due to financial pressures. The associated stress reactions are comparable to those of our ancestors. Stress leads us to react based on our intuition and to make decisions instinctively. The part of our brain that governs these reactions is the amygdala, which can quickly access our subconscious knowledge.

So the decision comes down to fight, flight, or play dead. Flight, in the context of a complex problem, would mean calling in sick, quitting, delegating the task to someone else, or putting in a transfer request, for example. Playing dead would be procrastinating, refusing to work, or, again, even calling sick. So what does actually grappling with and solving a complex problem look like? Blind action usually doesn't lead to success, and there is not enough time for careful analysis – so the hope lies in simplification. We think that this will stave off the danger… but this is exactly where the problem lies.

 Complex tasks and problems cannot be resolved through simplification.

It is just plain impossible to resolve complex tasks in this manner. Before we go any further, however, let us distinguish between what is simple and what is complex.

Repeatable, comprehensible, and self-explanatory

Many of the processes that are implemented in organizations nowadays are good examples of simple contexts. They have features in common that add up to simplicity – namely, cause-and-effect relationships that are clear, transparent, and repeatable. In simple contexts, there is a single right method, answer, or solution. No one questions how a light switch works, for example. When it's switched "on", the light goes on; when it's switched "off", the light goes off. There is no room for discussion – the process is clear to everyone. The cause is the action taken, and the effect is the result.

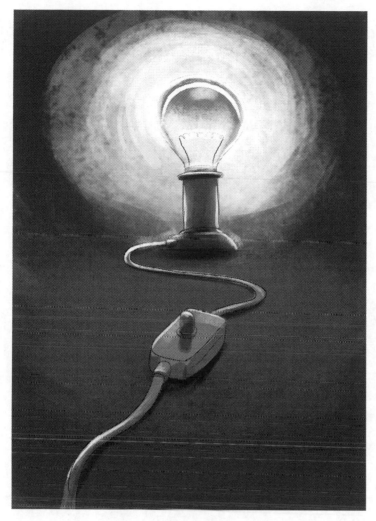

"It's simple!"

Let's say you signed a contract for the purchase for new office chairs, and the agreement provided that they would be delivered on March 15. Looking at your calendar today, you realize that it is already March 17. The delivery can be categorized as "late", and the manufacturer is thus in default. You can now respond accordingly with the measures provided for in the contract (late notice, cancellation of the order, etc.)

The key point here – and the difference between simple systems and complex ones – is predictability. Simple and complicated situations alike belong to an orderly world in which there is a clear relationship between cause and effect. This causal relationship exists in complex systems as well, but it can only be recognizedretrospectively. A simple system is characterized by a high degree of constraints, as illustrated and explained in the previous chapter. These govern our behavior and render it predictable; everyone knows what is right.

In simple contexts, categorization is the mechanism that enables us to make decisions.

Simplicity is the realm of "known knowns" – we know exactly what it is that we know. Everyone is clear about how things work. The relationships between causes and effects are comprehensible to all and require no discussion. This fosters stability. In such a system, a fact-based management style, in the sense of command and control, makes complete sense. Tasks can be easily delegated, and functions can be easily automated. Unfortunately, however, we also try to apply control where it makes no sense, or we stretch it too far.

One example of this is the tender process. Many companies' compliance guidelines provide that at least three bids from different suppliers must always be collected. Often, though, either the relevant department or the purchasing department already has a clear preference before the process is even begun. In such cases, the wording of the call for tenders itself may already make obvious to which supplier it is actually directed. Their two competitors are asked to submit bids only pro forma. The excessive control of this process results in people seeking workarounds to circumvent the process – which wastes a whole lot of energy and resources on all sides.

 Too much control just results in people trying to find ways around it.

We have a tendency to deem relationships "simple" even when they are far from it. We often think that we can identify clear cause-and-effect relationships in complex contexts, failing to realize that such connections can only be formulatedretrospectively.

In his book *Einfach managen: Komplexität vermeiden, reduzieren und beherrschen* ("Manage simply: Avoid, reduce, and control complexity") (Brandes, 2013), a former manager of the German supermarket company Aldi describes one of his consulting missions with a Turkish entrepreneurial group in 1995. They wanted to conquer Turkey with their chain of grocery stores, using the same principles by which Aldi had taken over Germany. The criteria for success – location, product range, and price – are described in a clear, self-evident, cause-and-effect manner: If correct choices are made for these criteria, then the store will be a success.

The author further describes how the first store was set up. Friends were sent shopping, and were to pick up products that they would expect to find at a grocery store. These products were laid out on the floor, to be cleverly arranged in a manner that would give customers a good "run-through" of the store. The planners then removed any duplicate products and added whatever was still missing. Within a week, the store was open for business. "This was a truly simple and very efficient process," in the author's opinion.

I will not dispute the efficiency of this process, but it certainly was not simple (in the sense in which this term is used in this book). Rather, it was pragmatic. Experience has, of course, testified to the fact that location, product range, and price are extremely important to the success of a supermarket. However, retail is and will remain a complex system, and one cannot predict success in the industry. With hindsight, it is easy to identify causality and market it as a priori knowledge. But this has nothing to do with simplicity – just as the steps taken in this case ultimately had nothing to do with simplicity either. The author and his colleagues experimented – and in several different ways. First of all, they brought together the products using the different ideas of the participants. They also experimented with the arrangement of the products. Basically, they carried out a "store success" experiment – and no one could have seriously guaranteed in advance that it would, indeed, be a success.

 The mere fact that a causal relationship has been repeated multiple times is no guarantee that it will be repeated the next time – nor does it render a complex matter simple.

The causality trap

On the morning of November 19, 2013, two people died in a helicopter crash near the German town of Neuhausen ob Eck, during what should have been a normal flying lesson for a 48-year-old flight instructor and his student. "Accident almost certainly caused by human error", a local newspaper reported after the crash analysis. After this "insight" was presented to readers right at the start, the article went on to explain that investigators could find nothing that suggested technical problems.

In other words, we have absolutely no idea what happened in that helicopter. But our need to always know the cause behind everything is so great that we end up citing "human error" in the event of an accident, even when the truth is that we just don't know – now that we have our causality, however, we can rest easy. The causality trap is especially critical in this case, as it is accompanied by a moral judgement and an assignment of guilt.

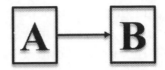

Clear cause, clear effect

The committee charged with investigating the Fukushima nuclear disaster concluded that human error was behind the ostensibly avoidable accident. One certainly does not need to be a complexity specialist to see that the "Fukushima system" is highly complex – even without considering the human factor. There were certainly mistakes, bad decisions, and lapses in judgment on the part of the TEPCO company, the regulatory authorities, and the government – none of this will be denied here. However, there was no simple chain of causes and effects that brought about this catastrophe in a linear manner.

When the primary waves of the Tohoku earthquake reached the Fukushima nuclear power plant at about 2:46 PM (local time) on March 11, 2011, it triggered the quick shutdown of reactors 1 to 3; the other reactors were not operating at the time due to maintenance work. The reactors' turbines shut down at about 2:48 PM. Pipes were damaged by the quake, water was leaking, and cooling circuits may have already been disabled at this time.

Fukushima 1 – the oldest and most powerful of Japan's nuclear power plants, with six generating units – was not connected to the nation's tsunami warning system. At 3:27 PM, the first tsunami wave – four meters high – reached the power plant. The plant's protective seawalls were 5.7 meters high; the seawater pumps behind them, however, got damaged. The waves that followed reached as high as 15 meters – flooding the reactors under up to five meters of water. The emergency power sources were damaged. The pressure in the reactors increased. The delivery of generators was delayed due to heavy traffic; the reactors had to be cooled in a makeshift fashion for several weeks.

This is just a brief sketch of what was a nuclear disaster of unfathomable proportions. One of the first questions that was asked after the catastrophe was: How could this have happened? People always seek the cause behind any such occurrence, and then see who was responsible. We always want to know the reason why things have happened. In this instance (and many others), the diagnosis of "human error" is an all-too-simple and putatively safe answer. But such a complex system is composed of reciprocal interrelationships – not linear causalities. And then there are also the massive external influences (earthquakes, tsunamis) and the relevant marginal conditions (seawall height, maintenance work, traffic, etc.) If we try to boil such contexts down to a simple cause-and-effect relationship, then we have fallen into the causality trap.

 We expect causality – and assume that similar causes will have similar effects.

We often discover causes very quickly, enabling us to quickly assign responsibility and guilt. For some people, the cause-and-effect principle is so deeply rooted in their thinking that sometimes they not only fail to see the real cause, but even see causes that do not actually exist. Konrad Lorenz calls the expectation of causality one of our "inborn teachers". (Lorenz, 1997)

This dependence on causality is not limited to Turkish supermarkets and nuclear disasters – it is reflected in all of our working life encounters, even in company management. We immediately and definitively know, for example, that our coworker has been absent-minded lately "because his wife is stressing him out." Another coworker doesn't have the report ready yet "because she doesn't have control over her department." And it's clear to us that "the boss is just telling us to do this now because…"

Our prejudices and stereotypes also come to the forefront with these cause-and-effect constructs – but what matters to us is simply that we have an explanation. We have a reason why. As managers and leaders, you are expected to be able to identify, manage, control, and account for your numbers, perspectives, goals, risks, indicators, and staff at any time – and you are expected to do so using simple causal relationships. This makes things simple, and simple is good. So, clearly, among your responsibilities is the balancing act between mastering complexity and simplifying matters for upper management.

> *"The strategy of genesis, I maintain, knows causal connection chains only on the small scale and only networks of causes as a whole. And nothing in the real world can be explained from one direction alone, but rather only from the context of a system of effects of which it itself is one."*
> RUPERT RIEDL

Simplicity: the fast track to chaos

Simple systems are orderly, stable, and transparent. At first glance, this appears to be a highly desirable state of affairs. It seems like complex and complicated systems should always be converted into simple ones – simple just seems *safe*. But appearances are deceptive: Simple, straightforward systems can easily slip into chaos if too much self-assuredness and self-complacency sets in.

In teams that work together over the long term, self-complacency tends to increase over time. The team members know each other well and understand each other. The working relationship is seen as harmonic and uncomplicated. Clear, agreed-upon rules and values are in place. The team members harness their potential, with a high comfort level and reduced resistance. The team now strives to preserve this state of affairs – perhaps even valuing the status quo above such things as innovation and advancement. In a prior book of mine, I addressed this situation in the context of project management; however, it can be understood universally, and carried over to other organizational contexts as well.

 A team that wallows in a "clear-and-defined" state runs the risk of getting stuck in its assumptions, patterns, and beliefs – and tends towards oversimplification.

Such a team is an accident waiting to happen. Any strong impetus may be enough to turn the system on its head and plunge it into chaos. Restructuring, corporate acquisitions or sell-offs, interpersonal conflicts, departures of individual team members, or a change in team leadership may be enough of an impulse – and the team no longer has sufficient flexibility or solution-finding mechanisms to adequately respond to the situation. Real crisis management is now necessary in order to get the team back on its feet and refocused.

Simple rules in complex systems

There is one simple thing that we do need in order to more successfully manage in complex systems: rules. Rules provide the constraints that govern a system's behavior, and which are in turn influenced by the system's behavior – a reciprocal relationship that does not exist in truly simple systems. Nature provides examples for us here too – let's take a look at how schools of fish are organized. Schools of fish are complex systems. They are self-organized, without any central leadership. Rather, they have simple, clear rules that facilitate the highly complex behavior of the fish within their large groups.

In addition to self-organization, schools of fish are characterized by a high level of adaptability. Their quick reactions to external impulses are especially impressive. In the event the school is attacked, the attacker gets confused and deceived – which gives individual fish a much higher chance of survival than if they were alone. This only works if the school swims as a single "object", which renders it more difficult for the attacker to make out each individual fish. In schools of fish, as well as in flocks of birds, certain rules are followed by all:

➢ *Keep the same distance from other fish.*
➢ *Keep the same speed as those around you.*
➢ *Avoid collisions.*

The rules are so simple – yet the resulting behaviors are so complex. Some species of fish divide their school in two, forcing the attacker to choose a portion to follow. Others swim behind the attacker, while yet others swim apart in an orderly manner. No individual fish makes, announces, and implements a decision. The fish influence each other's behaviors, as those with information about the attacker stimulate the others to act. The school's activity needs to reach a critical mass of about 5%, after which it continues intensifying.

So what does this mean for working together with others? In complex environments, do we need a few simple rules? Yes, that is exactly what it's all about. The mission statements that adorn our companies' walls can be a start. But you may have seen mission statements that are too roughly formulated, trying to cover too many things at the same time. Their effect quickly fizzles out – if they ever have any effect at all.

What doesn't get enough attention nowadays, in my experience, is the process by which basic rules are negotiated and established. Rules get created automatically, as soon as at least two people meet. We quickly learn what is okay and what is not okay in a company, picking up most of this non-verbally in the form of tacit rules. One superficial example would be the rule about lateness to meetings. What's it like at your company? Can you arrive late to a meeting? Such things can be simply observed – and quickly learned. If some co-workers arrive late, and this behavior is neither discussed nor censured nor does it have any other effect whatsoever on the meeting (e.g., other participants waiting), then one knows that one can arrive late. The first rule has been registered.

 It's not only the "what" – the "how" matters too.

This includes mutual expectations. Unfortunately, I repeatedly encounter managers who have not clearly formulated what they expect of their employees, nor do they know what their employees expect of them. There are always expectations when people work together with others. Your employees have clear ideas about how you should manage them, as well as about how their coworkers should work together with them. In order to cooperate constructively, it is essential that everyone knows what is expected of them. This is the only way that you will be able to respond to these expectations. And in the event that you are unwilling or unable to fulfill certain expectations, then it is essential that you make this known and, if necessary, find alternatives.

Sharing a dialogue about the rules necessary for a team also helps ensure that everyone understands things the same way. Communicating with each other regarding the key elements of their cooperation (e.g., criticisms, feedback, etiquette, openness, etc.) leads people to ultimately share a common understanding in these regards. Otherwise, what often happens is that different people end up using the same term or concept in different ways. Open communication, however, solves this problem.

> **Keep in mind the following:**
>
> ➢ Promote active discourse among your team members.
> ➢ Use this discourse to make implicit rules explicit.
> ➢ Clarify what your employees expect of you.
> ➢ Formulate your own expectations of your employees.
> ➢ Specify what will happen if rules are broken.

While we are on the topic of rules: managers are always complaining about employees who break rules. If this is something that you can relate to as well, then I suggest you take a look at yourself. How well do you stick to your company's rules? Do you make an occasional "exception" yourself? Often, I have even found managers boasting in front of their employees about rules that they have broken – generally rules that are irrelevant to those employees (e.g., with regard to the company car). If you set an example of rule-breaking, then do not be surprised if your employees follow that example. Your employees' behavior is guided by your leadership – do not underestimate your impact as a "role model".

Manage simply – instead of simplifying

No management situation is entirely simple, entirely complicated, or entirely complex. There are usually several different components. Thus, the first key step is distinguishing between them.

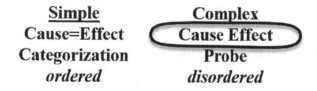

Make decisions *correctly*.

At this point, let's focus on simple contexts – and your responsibilities when a situation or problem is truly simple. Make sure that "clean processes" are established – you can achieve efficiencies here and utilize best-practice approaches. Tasks can be easily delegated, and clear, direct communication is in order.

You should also make sure that your team does not become self-complacent. Shared perspectives and beliefs should occasionally be critically questioned: "Is our simple way of looking at ourselves and our environment still relevant?" Be attentive. Be aware that increased certainty and productivity mean decreased resiliency for your organization. Even if it may seem like clear statements and astute delegation of tasks will allow you to remain largely hands-off, you should still maintain good contact with your employees. Find a middle path between micromanaging and just letting everything run on its own – and always look inward as well.

 In simple contexts, one can utilize best-practice solutions.

It is also important to check the environment for possible impulses that could lead to severe changes or chaos. You cannot prevent processes such as corporate acquisitions, restructuring, product discontinuations, or the like from triggering critical situations. But you *can* prepare yourself as early as possible to be able to respond quickly and correctly. Every change or crisis is foreshadowed in some manner – it's just that all too often we do not see or pay attention to this.

In our (corporate) culture, we are used to responding strongly to strong signals and weakly to weak signals. This is something that you should change. So-called "high reliability organizations" serve as a model in this regard – they operate under constant pressure, where errors could quickly lead to fatal consequences, thus they continually strive to pay attention to even the weakest signals. In order for you to do this in practice, you will need to train yourself to be aware – to be aware of your own perceptions, to be aware of your intuitions with regard to your colleagues, and to be aware of your intuitions with regard to your environment.

 It is particularly when we work in simple, stable contexts that we tend to regard events as singular moments.

Such events, however, may foreshadow things that will rock the system. *But we have risk management in place*, you may now be thinking. Risk management is good – but it is not enough. Classical risk management normally looks only at what is likely, and only within the limited time horizon of the planning cycle. In order to be able to pay attention and respond to weaker signals, however, the time period under observation must be expanded. Some companies in the insurance industry that have installed an early warning system for this purpose.

"Everything should be made as simple as possible, but not simpler."
ALBERT EINSTEIN

With its SONAR (systematic observation of notions associated with risk) system, Swiss Re has implemented an early warning system that enables it to identify, evaluate, and manage emerging risks, after collecting early (weak) signals of potential risks through its network of specialists. In this context, an emerging risk is a newly developing or changing risk which is difficult to quantify and which may have a major impact on the insurance industry, and thus on Swiss Re. The time frame for which these emerging risks and their effects are observed ranges from one to three to more than ten years.

One example of a risk that might only make its presence felt much later is that of a prolonged power blackout. Risk assessments normally consider the possibility of blackouts up to a few hours – but a terrorist attack, for example, could lead to a longer-term power outage. Thus, the SONAR system considers such a risk as well. Swiss Re makes clear that this risk has never materialized on a broad scale in the past – however, its extent in the future remains uncertain and thus it is worth observing. Other risk areas examined by SONAR are, for example, social unrest, mad cow disease, alcoholic lemonades, and nanotechnology. The question that drives such an early warning system is not the probability of each different risk event, but rather what our future might look like. Sketching out scenarios for an alternative future, along with action options for the worst-case scenario, is quite helpful, providing an outstanding training opportunity against self-complacency.

SUMMING UP:

- ❖ Simplification is not a strategy that can reduce complexity.
- ❖ Simple systems can be predicted; there is always a single correct answer.
- ❖ Our desire for cause-and-effect relationships leads us into the causality trap.
- ❖ Simple systems can collapse into chaos quite easily.
- ❖ A complex system needs simple rules.
- ❖ Staying attentive helps keep simple systems stable.

Misconception #2:
Complex is the same
as complicated

More than four years late, three billion Euros over budget, and full of shady dealings and missed commitments – the repeatedly delayed construction of the new Berlin Brandenburg Airport continues to get Germans all worked up. And what has supposedly been the cause of all the problems? The fire protection system. "It is not ready yet because it is too complex," the lead engineer told the state parliament's inquiry committee.

I rolled my eyes when I read this. *Again this confusion between "complex" and "complicated"*, I thought. A fire protection system is a technical construct – it cannot be complex. Rather, it is complicated. Does it have dynamics? Interconnectedness, with reciprocal relationships? Can it change without any external influence? Is it non-transparent? Absolutely not! Even I – certainly a non-expert with regard to fire protection systems – could eventually understand the equipment, if I were to dedicate myself to it intensively enough.

Confusion between what is "complex" and what is "complicated" has been common for quite some time. Complexity has become a buzzword that gets applied liberally to describe many different causes, problems, challenges, or characteristics – often without regard to the actual meaning of the word. And the same thing happens in reverse – complex matters routinely get called "complicated". To give just one well-known example, French philosopher Jean-Paul Sartre has been quoted as saying, "In football, everything is complicated by the presence of the opposite team."

Whoops. At most, perhaps the *rules* of the sport can be considered complicated – although even the rules of football are ultimately quite simple. The sport itself, however, is highly *complex*. Or do you think you can predict the course of play between two teams? Highly doubtful. There are twenty-two "direct" participants on the field at any given time, each interacting with all of the other participants, as well as receiving stimuli from the referees – and then there are also external factors, such as the weather, coaches, strategies, etc. Predicting football? Impossible – it's completely unpredictable.

"Complex" sounds more serious than "complicated". *Oh, your assignment is just complicated? Mine is complex – I've got it much tougher!* When something is complicated, we feel like we can get a get a grip on it by analyzing it properly. But when something is complex, it has a whiff of inscrutability and abstruseness. It's more striking – tell someone that "it's a very complex matter," and they just can't come back with any arguments. This makes it easier to hide our own lack of knowledge – both in complicated situations that we haven't fully grasped yet, and in complex situations that we never fully will.

You may now be thinking that people might lump "complex" and "complicated" together intentionally. Yes, this may happen as well. However, in most cases, it is simply due to the fact that we are unable to distinguish between the two. Very few people have truly sweated over what actually lies behind these terms. They think that "complex" must be just a step up from "complicated". Complicated 2.0, so to speak. And thus, it is suddenly possible for dialogues, Excel spreadsheets, photographs, or even databases to be considered "complex".

The lead engineer on the Berlin airport project is far from alone in confusing these terms. One can find treasure chests full of gems in the relevant internet forums where people deal with this topic:

- "Even if the problem is complex, there can be a simpler solution." (Username *Dr. Bakterius*, www.mikrocontroller.net forums)
- "The concept of complexity itself is complex, and it's difficult to explain it in an uncomplicated way." (Username *Jonny Obivan*, www.mikrocontroller.net forums)
- Complexity is inherently something that is complicated in different ways for different individuals." (Username *Juri Parallelowitsch*, www.mikrocontroller.net forums)

It's not all that bad, you say? Well, if it were to only manifest itself in press conference answers, then I would agree. Beyond this linguistic confusion, however, there is usually also confusion or indifference with regard to the appropriate measures to actually be taken in response to different problems. Complex and complicated are not merely two different concepts – they come from two entirely different worlds, and problems from one of these worlds cannot be solved using measures from the other. If the responsible parties of the Berlin airport project do, in fact, see the fire protection problem as a complex task and work on it in a corresponding manner, then I am certain that this airport will never be completed.

Complex is not the same as complicated

Why is it, in fact, that we confuse the terms "complicated" and "complex" and use them incorrectly? Because these terms are not distinctly defined in terms of our colloquial usage. Definitions that are comprehensible but incorrect have taken hold in our vernacular. We deem things, problems, or tasks to be "complicated" when they have many components or parts that are somehow dependent upon one another. We see a system as "complicated" when it is large and confusing, although we get the feeling that we can work it out. On the other hand, we refer to things that we just cannot comprehend as "complex". Our usual distinction is thus based on the question of whether it is something that we can understand or not.

If I were to suggest to you that a coffee machine should be categorized as "complicated", you would probably agree with me. It is a technical device, consisting of a manageable number of parts, and has a clearly defined purpose and a handy size. We have no problems dealing with it, even if we are not electronics experts. On the other hand, if I were to suggest to you that an Airbus A380 should be categorized as merely "complicated", you might feel that this is not a strong enough word to describe it. Doesn't one really need to be an expert to understand an Airbus A380? That's true – but it is also true that any one of us could become such an expert. The number of parts is larger than in a coffee machine, and there are significantly more dependencies between them, but even an airplane is ultimately still just a technical piece of equipment.

It is really just a matter of time and intensive study before any person could grasp the workings of an Airbus, and each person has a subjective sense of how easy or difficult it would be for him to gain an understanding of the aircraft if he were to dedicate himself to studying it intensively. The more difficult and tedious this seems, the more likely a person would call it "complex". It thus becomes rather more an expression of our own sensitivities than an actual description of the system itself. In order to dispel the misconception that complicated and complex are basically the same, we need to establish a clear and accurate distinction between them.

"Everything's in order": Features of complicated systems

More than 27 million taxpayers in Germany are governed by German tax law. It has undergone almost a dozen recent reforms, with changes that have affected myriad provisions. Germany's tax law comprises more than 200 different tax statutes and totals more than 100,000 legal provisions – far too much for a "normal" taxpayer to grasp. How many Germans do you think are aware of the fact that a reduced VAT rate is applicable for pacemakers and prosthetics, but the full VAT rate is applicable for their replacement parts and accessories? Or that a reduced rate is applicable for eggs and egg yolks, although not for non-edible eggs without shells or for non-edible egg yolks? There are a ton of exceptions and special rules, exceptions to the exceptions – and, of course, exceptions to these latter exceptions as well.

This is why tax advising is such a bustling industry in the country, with more than 75,000 accountants working as experts in the field. A complicated tax system has advantages too, offering plenty of loopholes. Starbucks, for example, was operating in Great Britain for 15 years without paying a single cent of corporate income tax, despite the fact that its branches there were successful and generated good profits. On an ongoing basis, each branch remitted about 6 percent of its revenues to the company's European headquarters in the Netherlands as an intellectual property licensing fee – and this exempted them from their corporate income tax obligations in Great Britain. What might be the purpose behind such a licensing fee? At the same time, Starbucks was substantially exempted from taxes in the Netherlands because its European headquarters were located there. By now, however, the company has moved its European headquarters to London, which plugged up the loophole. These examples demonstrate how tax law – almost anywhere in the world – can seem tortuous, arcane, and incomprehensible. Why, then, is it not complex – but rather "merely" complicated?

Analyses lay the groundwork for decisions.

Complicated systems, situations, or problems can be easily distinguished from others once one is aware of their pertinent features.

 The key feature of complicated systems is the existence of clear cause-and-effect relationships.

These cause-and-effect relationships can be identified in advance. Laws – including tax laws – consist broadly of causalities that have been defined by humans. If I distribute gifts to my most loyal clients, then I can deduct the costs of these gifts for tax purposes – this is unambiguous and predictable. This particular circumstance is not yet complicated – however, the multitude of regulations eventually makes matters so. Although there are clear cause-and-effect relationships in a complicated system, these are not one-dimensional – i.e., there may be several different paths towards a single result. In the above example, I would ask my tax advisor which regulations are most beneficial to me, as he is an expert in these very matters.

In other words: There may be several correct solution paths, but the results are already determined even before the matter is analyzed by an expert – and the more profound the expert's knowledge of the particular set of facts, the "simpler" the relationships between them will seem. Complicated matters are the domain of experts. They analyze the system, finding possible solution paths. My tax accountant, for example, scours the tax laws for deductions that relate to client gifts and that can be applied to my situation. And then, perhaps, we come to a decision together regarding how to file this information with the tax authorities.

Analysis is thus the mechanism that enables us to make decisions regarding complicated matters. When we know little or nothing about a complicated subject, it seems to overwhelm us – and so, we may like to call it "complex". However, it is and remains only complicated, if it remains part of that orderly world in which clear cause-and-effect relationships can be identified. This is the world in which we are most comfortable. From the time we start school, we learn that the best way to solve problems is by analyzing them, and that a clear cause-and-effect relationship can be found for almost anything – it's a pity that we don't also learn how disorderly the world can be, and how to find a solution when it is. More on that later in this chapter.

 Analysis is our decision-making mechanism in complicated contexts.

If the complicated world is the realm of experts, then this naturally has an effect on how we manage. On one hand, well-established experts are sometimes divas with certain expectations regarding how they will be interacted with if they are to deliver peak performance. On the other hand, you as a manager need to be aware of how easy it is for you (along with your team, department, or organization) to fall into the "expert trap". When reviewing lessons learned from unsuccessful projects, the most common diagnosis is that: "We should have brought in more/different/better experts." We are often convinced that expertise is the answer to all questions, problems, or difficulties. We believe in expertise – oh, if only we had asked someone who really understands this area! Look at the yellow pages – we are willing to pay for deep expert knowledge and to actively seek out the experts. And the deeper and more detailed an expert's knowledge, the more "important" that expert and his opinion.

Do you have some proven experts on your own team? Good, then take a closer look. Some experts get too full of themselves and their own importance, which leads them to start shutting out other opinions and perspectives. Colleagues who are new or who come from other fields are either not taken seriously or are simply ignored. In the views of these experts, such colleagues have not yet attained a suitable level of expertise in the relevant matter, and thus have no right to discuss it with them as equals. It sometimes even goes so far as the expert declaring certain facts or problems "non-existent" simply because he would have to look outside of his own knowledge silo; as far as this expert is concerned, what he doesn't know just doesn't exist.

"Expect the unexpected": Complex systems cannot be predicted

Making decisions and leading employees are always essential tasks of managers, regardless of whether the context is complicated or complex. So how can we operate successfully when we leave behind the well-ordered, complicated world to instead occupy ourselves with complex contexts? Do we need to modify our own personal management strategies? An example from nature is helpful here.

Bright butterflies, exotic birds, and flowers in every color combination imaginable. A green sea of mosses, ferns, vines, and towering trees. We're in the Southeast Asian rainforest, the third-largest in the world. At 60 million years old, it is also the oldest rainforest in the world, with substantial forest areas remaining in Indonesia, Myanmar, and Papua New Guinea.

For us westerners, the region is a treasure trove of exotic flora and fauna. The Sumatran rhinoceros, the most critically endangered member of the rhinoceros family, roams these forests, as do the clouded leopard, proboscis monkey, and orangutan. The region is also home to the strangler fig, the rafflesia (the largest parasitic plant on earth), and the carnivorous pitcher plant. On Borneo, the indigenous inhabitants are known as the "Dayak", consisting of many different groups that each have their own different languages and traditions – in other words, many different participants. Roughly, the main task of the rainforest is to limit the greenhouse effect, converting carbon dioxide into oxygen; one result of rainforest destruction is that the carbon dioxide concentration rises accordingly.

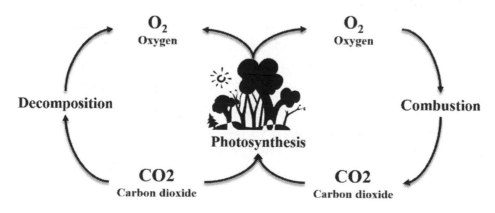

Effects and countereffects mean dynamics.

Another key function of this ecosystem is storing water and releasing it through evaporation. Essential to the rainforest are the interrelationships and symbiotic relationships among its parts – these have developed over millions of years and are defining characteristics of the ecosystem. The loss of one species can dramatically affect another species' chances of survival.

A good example of this can be found with the Brazil nut in the rainforests of Central and South America. Its continued existence is dependent upon a ground-dwelling rodent called the agouti – no other animal in the area has teeth that are sharp enough to crack open the Brazil nut's shell. The agouti does not eat all the seeds – it also buries many of them all around. Some of these seeds then germinate, growing up as the next generation of Brazil nut trees. Another animal is responsible for the pollination of Brazil nut trees – the orchid bees, without which the trees could not survive. This is another clear, simple example of the interrelationships that exist in the tropics.

In some cases, the survival of both participants is dependent upon such relationships. Ants, for example, are particularly adept at this – in addition to their interactions with plants, fungi, and other insects, their relationships with caterpillars are also quite exceptional. A gland on the back of one particular species of caterpillar produces a sweet chemical substance that serves as food for the ants; in exchange, the ants provide these caterpillars with protection and shelter.

> *"Trying to predict the future is like trying to drive down a country road at night with no lights while looking out the back window."*
> PETER DRUCKER

It is easy to imagine the sorts of effects that are brought about by changes or disturbances to the rainforest system. All of the reciprocal relationships and interactions amongst the elements of the system must adapt if, for example, an agricultural project diverts the flow of water or if climatic changes occur – or anything else of the sort. This complex system is more than the sum of its parts. The direct relationship between the agouti and the Brazil nut tree can be easily explained by experts and described in cause-and-effect terms – but for the entire rainforest system, we must also consider all of the ensuing interrelationships. What happens if the agouti stops distributing seeds? What do the resulting vegetation changes mean for other plants and animals? The effects of one change are thus always determined by many other dynamic factors.

Only retroactively can cause-and-effect relationships be described in complex systems.

Most situations in our organizations are complex. They involve changes and unpredictability. This may include new management or a reorganization of the company's operations or the launch of a new product.

So what are the key features of complex systems and situations, in contrast with complicated systems? The distinguishing feature that is both quite frightening and extremely important is the lack of predictability. A complex system cannot be fully described in advance – neither its behavior nor what will happen to it in the future. The cause-and-effect relationships can only be discovered and formulated in retrospect.

In retrospect, it is possible to say whether a new product on the market has led to an increase in sales. In retrospect, we can tell whether the reorganization of a business has had the desired results. In retrospect, we know what effects a change in management has brought about. Even if we are firmly convinced that we can predict what will happen in these situations, this is nothing more than an illusion – and one that is hard for us to let go. Doing so requires us to acknowledge that making decisions in complex systems does not require the use of analysis – but rather experiments.

Experiments? Yes, you read correctly. In contexts where we can no longer determine causes and effects in advance, we have no other choice besides testing (⇒ Glossary) and experimentation. We can then observe the results and take decisions that are geared towards reinforcing positive results or mitigating negative results. We gather experience, which we can then put to use in the next round of experimentation. There are, however, no guarantees of any precise results.

 When cause and effect can no longer be determined in advance, then we must experiment.

Let's take a look at Apple Inc., a company that stands for success and innovation. For most people, the first Apple products that will come to mind are the iPhone, iPad, iPod, or MacBook – all of which have been highly successful in the market. These products all form part of an overall concept. Needless to say, Apple is following a clear product strategy. But Apple has also had plenty of less successful ventures. The first "Apple phone" was not the iPhone, but rather the "Rokr".

which hit the market in 2005 with a capacity to sync up to 100 songs via iTunes; one year later, however, Apple refocused its efforts. Likewise, in 1992, Apple collaborated with IBM to develop a common operating system, founding the company Taligent (a portmanteau of the words "talent" and "intelligent") towards this end; the project never gained traction, Apple withdrew from the project in 1995, and the company was quietly dissolved.

In that same year, Apple dabbled in video game consoles, with the company's "Pippin" marketed by other companies under license – it flopped. And do you remember the Power Mac G4 Cube? Steve Jobs spoke of this cube-based machine as the pinnacle of computer design – launched in 2000, the model was already discontinued in 2001. The list of unsuccessful Apple product experiments goes on.

Complex matters are non-linear and unpredictable.

The key point here is that successfully bringing products to the market is a thoroughly complex challenge. No one can seriously claim to be able to predict success or failure. "We knew it," is a statement that can only be made and justified in retrospect – once the cause-and-effect relationships have become clear. A hundred songs on a cell phone are not enough for users – accordingly, the Rokr was rejected. A cube-shaped computer that costs significantly more than other models won't be embraced by customers – accordingly, the G4 Cube was too expensive and was rejected.

We examine our successes and failures to guide our future strategy – and this often brings us success, although sometimes not. It is not a question of having the right or wrong strategy, but rather is due to the nature of complex systems – we are always smarter with hindsight. To look at it purely as a question of strategy would mean that we see the matter as predictable, and would thus presume that Apple will inevitably be successful with all of its "iProducts" in the future by following its strategy. This may end up being the case – but in order for it to happen, Apple must constantly remain adaptive and experimental, because the market and the company's customers are neither static nor predictable.

Attempting to resolve complex matters in the same manner as we resolve complicated matters is neither a formula for success nor a recipe for incubating innovations and new products. This is where changing the thinking of managers and executives is most difficult. It is difficult for many people to leave aside the orderly, predictable world and instead use testing and experimentation as decision-making tools, as this does not fit in with the management thinking that has become so ingrained over the course of recent decades.

 The first key step towards changing one's thinking lies in accepting complexity as complexity – with all that this entails.

Managing the complicated and the complex

The foregoing observations have made clear that complex and complicated are not the same, but rather occupy two entirely different worlds. This, of course, has a significant effect on decision-making and on leading one's employees. So how, then, can one meaningfully lead employees in these two different contexts? To start with, every manager needs to be able to distinguish between them.

Complicated
Cause → Effect
Analyze
ordered

Complex
Cause Effect
Probe
disordered

Confusing the two has serious consequences.

In your day-to-day managing life, you are often faced with complicated tasks and problems. You need to determine which experts will carry out which analyses. You are probably not the best technical expert on your team or in your company for every single situation, but this does not matter – just ask whoever knows the subject better. Your experts will identify for you all of the possibilities to be analyzed and studied. They will define boundaries like the budget, time frame, and possible solutions. You will undoubtedly know in advance the criteria by which you will end up choosing among these solutions – price, timing, aesthetics, simplicity, and so on. This is how we solve problems with which we are familiar, and which do not contain anything new or special. At the same time, there are some challenges when managing experts – and the next chapter will discuss how to deal with these challenges. Here, though, we will focus on managing in complex situations and systems.

"That which gives the extraordinary firmness to our belief in causality is not the great habit of seeing one occurrence following another but our inability to interpret events otherwise than as events caused by intentions."
FRIEDRICH NIETZSCHE

Are most of the employees on your team specialists with detailed, in-depth knowledge of their areas of expertise? This is obviously great, but it also presents you with a challenge. Some experts have difficulties in complex domains. They sometimes do not deal well with uncertainties and unpredictability, because they are used to always having clarity and being able to resolve things via analysis. Experts who lack all-around skills will be overwhelmed if you declare that decisions will instead be made based on experimentation from now on. But part of working in complex realms is always seeking out new, previously unknown solutions.

 You can change your experts' mental model by no longer asking "Will it work?" – but rather "How can it work?"

A scene from the film *Apollo 13* offers a clear example of this. Experts, under intense time pressure, needed to find a way to connect a CO2 filter to the lunar module's air filtration system. The problem was that the filter was round and the receptacle was square – and even as a non-expert, I can tell you that this just won't work! However, such an answer was unacceptable in this case, as the survival of the three astronauts in the lunar module depended upon solving this problem. So the experts were faced with the unenviable task of finding a solution from amongst the materials available on the spacecraft – and fast. In the end, these experts managed to figure out a way to make the connection using spacesuits and plastic parts.

At our own workplaces, we are not always under pressures as intense as those faced by the Mission Control Center experts in *Apollo 13*. But there are still certain aspects you should always consider when forming teams or groups. When solving complex tasks, you also need generalists as a counterbalance to your specialized experts. Although generalists are not at home in the detail levels of knowledge silos, they can make connections more easily and be more attentive to interrelationships. And often enough, a naïve question due to a lack of in-depth knowledge can end up being a stimulus for new and innovative ideas.

Managing in complex contexts clearly does not involve telling your employees how to proceed. This is something that you will never be able to do sufficiently – nor should you.

Managing in complex contexts rather involves creating the "right" environment and assessing the system.

To achieve an optimal environment in complex situations, you must set the right guidelines and rules. With a set of clear, transparent, and comprehensible rules, you will facilitate your system's self-organization. There should be a manageable number of simple rules. This framework of rules then provides for self-regulation, just like in schools of fish or flocks of birds (as described in the previous chapter). Their simple rules include:

1. Move towards the midpoint of those whom you see around you.
2. Move away as soon as someone comes too close to you.
3. Move in approximately the same direction as those around you.

Obviously, there is no universally applicable framework of rules for managing in complex organizations. The particular simple rules that may guide your system to success are rules that you must determine individually and adapt constantly. No framework of rules should be rigidly defined and applied – when there are changes in the context or the team or any other circumstance, then the rules necessary for self-regulation may need to be adapted too. As a manager, you are usually granted a certain amount of leeway by your organization. Take advantage of this to define rules together with your team as much as possible. Specify the rules that you consider indispensable, and also take advantage of your leeway by allowing effective patterns to emerge through testing.

What to watch out for:

➢ In many organizations, it is difficult to utilize the terminology of complexity. Terms like "testing", "experimentation", and "non-transparency" are often simply not part of the organization's cultural vocabulary.
➢ Using other terminology allows you to be a sort of translator between the two worlds.
➢ Rather than prescribing a new approach, simply invite others to try it.
➢ This is true with regard to your staff and your management alike – basically for anyone who is not yet comfortable around the topic of complexity or who still has particular misconceptions about it.

I am often asked whether this really works and whether such an approach can really be taken with everyone. The answer is yes. A good example of self-organization is the consulting company Vollmer & Scheffczyk in Stuttgart.

This rather small firm is one of the few organizations in Germany that has employed such a model thus far. You will surely agree with me that the successful management of an engineering consulting company is a complex task, so let's take a closer look at this company's model.

Vollmer & Scheffczyk's management ascertained that, in the long run, the traditional bonus system model only resulted in the maximization of individual bonuses; based on this realization, they decided to take an entirely different route. At Vollmer & Scheffczyk, each employee sets his own salary. Moreover, each employee also determines independently how much vacation he will take and when. These details are transparent with respect to all who work at the company, and he must answer to the other employees accordingly. This naturally leads to the desired intensive discourse – and one's salary can indeed be reduced as a result. Anyone can review all company books and records at any time, so everyone is well aware of the company's situation. This fosters the individual responsibility of each employee, as they can see for themselves whether the company can afford their salary or their vacation.

Even with this structure, there are occasionally people who try to take advantage for their own benefit. But they soon either get removed from the system or leave of their own accord. In the long run, the type of people who latch onto and stay within this system are those who are interested in this sort of responsibility, are able to handle it, and are flexible. Obviously not everyone will be able to relate Vollmer & Scheffczyk's example to their own situations – it merely represents one of many possible paths. We will address the forms and structures of organizations in more detail in the chapter on misconception #9.

So, managing a complex organization primarily means fostering self-organization and self-regulation. The manager is the one who must assess and evaluate the system, and then intervene accordingly whenever necessary. Intervention is not geared towards reeling in individuals who deviate, but rather is more generally about correcting the overall direction of the system. The manager assesses whether the system is producing the appropriate results or is moving in the right direction for achieving its goals. The path towards these goals is not predetermined. And it is, of course, the employees on a team who discover this path and the relevant solutions. They must participate actively and be unafraid to offer ideas and try out different things – and they must be unafraid to sometimes fail.

Failure is a necessary agent for finding new solutions or developing innovations.

This is especially true at the start of a process, when an organization or team has a smaller pool of experience. When testing and experimentation are the decision-making mechanisms, then the goal should never be a series of experiments without any failures at all. This would imply a return to traditional command & control. The spectrum of experiments should always be so wide that failures and errors (i.e., undesired results) will inevitably be produced. Otherwise the testing will end up like a classic trial-and-error, simply processing one attempt after another. This can eventually get you into a quagmire, as a complex system will not wait for you – it will continue evolving as it desires, and perhaps even at a faster pace. All of this demands a lot from managers. They must be courageous, they must be able to handle uncertainty, they must be a link between two different worlds, and they must create a proper environment. The most important factors towards creating such an environment are summed up below:

> *Failures and errors are permitted.*
> *Discourse is possible and encouraged.*
> *Interconnectedness is permitted.*
> *Learning is possible and allowed.*

SUMMING UP:
- ❖ Complicated is not the same thing as complex.
- ❖ Complicated systems can be predicted. There may be several right answers or solutions.
- ❖ Complex systems can only retroactively be described in terms of their cause-and-effect relationships.
- ❖ In order for complex problems to be solved, errors must be made.
- ❖ Complex systems are self-organized, and self-organization requires clear, simple rules.

Misconception #3: The experts will figure everything out

During your most recent job search, what was the first thing you looked at in the job listings? Probably the list of skills and qualifications required, right? The first thing that you did was check out whether your own expertise matched what the company was seeking. Job titles usually give a general idea, but the "Required skills and qualifications" section is where it really becomes clear – companies always look to hire experts with deep knowledge in clearly defined areas of specialty.

So, let's say an automobile industry supplier is seeking a "Gear and Shaft Expert". Tasks for the position relate to the macro- and microgeometries of running gears as well as shaft-hub connections. Among the required qualifications are an engineering degree, expert knowledge of vehicle transmissions, and years of experience dealing with gear and shaft specifications (material selection, heat treatment, residual dirt, etc.) The company needs an expert.

It goes without saying that the job description will also mention requirements such as flexibility, commitment, an ability to work well under pressure, and an ability to work well in teams. But let's be honest – these are usually not much more than placeholders. The requirements relating to the candidate's expertise will generally be focused on in the job interview and will be scrutinized far more intensely. Every employer wants to avoid taking chances in this regard – if an "expert" gets hired but turns out to *not* actually be such an expert, that would really be the worst-case scenario for the company. So there is seldom much discussion of what flexibility, commitment, etc. really mean to the company, and whether these are things that you would actually bring to the position. Those are the "soft factors" – but what really counts are your technical qualifications in the field, right? These are what we put our faith in, and it will probably always be this way.

This makes me think of our high-ranking politicians here in Germany – how often do the ministers' cabinet positions actually match with their fields of professional expertise? There are even a few department-hoppers who just "minister away" at whatever positions are offered to them. (Incidentally, such job-hopping is highly frowned upon in "normal" jobs.) Let's take a look at Ursula von den Leyen's résumé, for example. She studied economics and medicine. Her first position in the federal government was as Minister of Family Affairs, Senior Citizens, Women, and Youth. She later served as Minister of Labor and Social Affairs, and is now Minister of Defense. At one point she was also offered to lead the health department, although she turned down the offer; her detractors say it's because it wouldn't get her as far politically.

But back to the issue of qualifications. At least in the case of the defense ministry, under a pure theory of proven expertise, I can see no argument for Ms. Von der Leyen to have been given her position. Economics and medicine have absolutely nothing at all to do with defense. But she is not alone – we also have a lawyer looking after Food and Agriculture, a grammar school teacher in charge of Economic Affairs and Energy, and a tax administration graduate now taking care of Family Affairs, Senior Citizens, Women, and Youth. Congratulations to our federal cabinet ministers on landing their jobs – in the "real" world, each of them would have been kicked out in the first round of interviews due to a lack of expertise in the field.

Maybe we shouldn't take such a narrow view of this – ultimately it's about politics, which involve really important and far-reaching decisions and strategies. These are not just any jobs in just any company; the priorities are set quite differently. Yet it's nice to see that expertise seems to have staying power once acquired, even if the environment changes – this makes not only the government's family policies more family-friendly, but rather the government itself.

Or maybe we've simply come to learn and accept that expertise isn't the only thing that's necessary to do a job well. We don't only need experts – we need generalists as well. Many companies seem to have realized this too, changing job posting titles from "XYZ Expert" to "XYZ Generalist".

So, for example, a large IT company recently sought an "IT Process Consulting Generalist". So far, so good – until you read the job description, which made clear that the candidate really needed to be a jack-of-all-trades. Job responsibilities ranged from sales support to conducting training workshops, and from running complex projects to portfolio management. Knowledge of current IT topics was required, of course, as well as a degree in the field and at least five years of professional experience.

And then came the list of required skills. If you figured that in-depth skills would not be required for this job, then think again – this "generalist" was actually required to have expertise in a variety of different methods and tools. So even in this case, what the company really wanted was far from a generalist – they were looking for an expert. Or more precisely, an "expert 2.0" – with a whole lot of skills to handle diverse tasks cutting across the entire field of IT.

It's a difficult situation – first, because experts want to work in their specific areas of expertise with clearly defined roles; second, because a generalist is a generalist and not a fine-tuned expert; and third, because the word generalist surely scares some candidates off. In a society that so strongly believes in expertise (at least outside of politics), no one wants to be the non-expert.

Let's not delude ourselves – how are job positions filled? On the basis of proven (i.e., printed on a sheet of paper) expertise. The first round of reviewing candidates is often handled by interns – because anyone can just check off the candidates' résumés against a list of required skills. We think that a person can only fill a role if he has the right expertise. We believe that he can only achieve good results if he has the right expertise. Can we only be successful if we have the right experts? Apparently, we have not yet understood.

Aren't we all experts?

In what area(s) are you an expert? I presume that you can come up with at least one answer to this question. We have all become experts, especially as we advance in our professional lives. We have all specialized in something. Depending on your academic path, this may have happened earlier or later – but eventually you have developed expertise in an area of business administration, law, computer science, medicine, motor vehicles, electronics, or some other field.

Throughout this time, you have consistently been told (especially through the media) that specialized experts are always in demand. Experts explain matters for reporters, journalists, and talk shows. They solve problems – even complicated ones. They stand out for their analytical abilities and their in-depth knowledge. So, you figure, gaining specialized expertise is important to your career path. After completing your studies, during which you have already specialized in a field, you start looking for a suitable job. The job descriptions are always looking for people with specific expertise. You feel like an expert in your area already, so you step right into a highly specialized role, and your skills are usually developed further as you perform your job. Your career path as an expert is now set and you will achieve everything for which you strive – recognition, career advancement, money, and influence.

We firmly believe that only experts can achieve good results in their jobs. Deep knowledge is necessary for solving problems and generating new ideas – this has been our thinking for decades. We grow up with this belief. It's how we are educated. And as our world has grown more complicated and specialized, we too have become more focused.

And that is a good thing. If you have some health problem, you will probably want to head straight for the relevant medical specialist, rather than to a general practitioner. Where do you bring your car when it makes strange noises? Probably to a manufacturer-certified repair shop. When it comes to sports, we seek out coaches who are specialized in our sport of choice. We read books by renowned experts – but we would never think of reading a book about HR strategies, for example, if it were written by someone who is not an expert in the field. We trust only experts – and this is true even with regard to ourselves.

Ultimately, experts have in-depth knowledge and the requisite understanding of their field. They are good analysts and are familiar with different solution possibilities. They can draw upon many years of experience with exactly the same sorts of problems in exactly the same subject area. This gives us a sense of security and the confidence that everything will work out fine. Certainly, expertise has its benefits. At the same, however, it is also the basis for a great misconception: that only experts can solve the complex problems of our times.

> *"Don't be swayed by an expert who tells you, 'I've been doing it this way for 20 years.' It's possible to do something wrong for 20 years."*
> KURT TUCHOLSKY

For experts, the world is always complicated

"Complicated" is the domain where experts feel at home. They resolve problems by analyzing them, using an "if… then…" thought pattern. Even if a task is quite complicated, an expert can deal with all the "ifs" and the "thens", thinking outside the box. The point here is: experts want things to be linear and predictable – i.e., complicated. We have already addressed the difference between complicated and complex, so I will make reference here only to the essential aspects.

Complicated matters

> *have clear cause-and-effect relationships,*
> *are predictable,*
> *can have several correct solutions,*
> *can be resolved via analysis, and*
> *require expert knowledge.*

The way that we have been trained to think about and solve problems is wonderfully suited for complicated tasks. And if the problem in question relates to our area of specialty, then we can bring all of our knowledge and experience to the table. As experts, we are comfortable on such terrain. And therein lies the crux: Experts are so accustomed to following this single linear thought pattern that it has become fully automated, and they thus pay no attention to whether the problem itself is complicated, complex, or perhaps even simple. But complex matters cannot be predicted; their cause-and-effect relationships become clear only in retrospect. Accordingly, analysis is no longer the appropriate decision-making instrument.

Within their areas of specialty, experts generally get the benefit of the doubt. We believe in their expertise, their knowledge, and their reliability, and this belief gives us a sense of certainty and comfort. And if a colleague who is a marketing expert analyzes what we need to do to expand our customer base, then (at least in our head) we give him full responsibility for this – if it doesn't work, then we're off the hook ourselves. Meanwhile, experts also satisfy our desire for simplicity, explaining to us how the world ticks and how to solve problems – it all sounds quite plausible, the analysis is convincing, and we can putatively find our bearings. We often consider experts infallible – but it is precisely in this regard that we need to be careful.

Even experts are sometimes wrong

Most of us seem to actually believe that experts are so well-versed in their areas of expertise that their prognoses and analyses are always on the mark. However, there are tons of examples to refute this assumption:

> ➤ *"Two years from now, spam will be solved."*
> BILL GATES, 2004

> ➤ *"Next Christmas, the iPod will be dead, finished, gone, kaput."*
> ALAN SUGAR, BRITISH BUSINESSMAN & MULTIMILLIONAIRE, 2005

> ➤ *"Email is a totally unsaleable product."*
> IAN SHARP, SHARP ASSOCIATES, 1979

> ➤ *"Television won't be able to hold on to any market it captures after the first six months. People will soon get tired of staring at a plywood box every night."*
> DARRYL F. ZANUCK, HEAD OF TWENTIETH CENTURY-FOX, 1946

> ➤ *"The horse is here to stay, but the automobile is only a novelty – a fad."*
> PRESIDENT OF MICHIGAN SAVINGS BANK, 1903

Just a few little gaffes, you're thinking? No, these are simply some of the most famous examples of the expert trap. Specialization, while admittedly important, has its price – which we pay by falling into several different thinking traps:

1. *Overconfidence*
   People tend to believe that they know more than they actually do. They overestimate themselves and their skills. The "overconfidence effect" also extends to one's ability to predict things. And experts, in particular, tend to overestimate themselves to even greater degrees, which often directly results in too-optimistic project planning. So, work with pessimistic scenarios.

2. *The illusion of control*
   "We've got everything under control," is a line that is heard often in offices and conference rooms. But is it really the case? Do we really have everything under control? Well, probably much less often than we would like. We tend to believe that we have an ability to control things, even when it is objectively impossible. This belief gives us a sense of certainty and self-regulation, even if our environment becomes chaotic and unpredictable. Make yourself aware of what you can actually control, and accept those things that are out of your control.

3. *Hindsight bias*

As experts, we believe that we are good at predicting and projecting within our field. It is our area of expertise, and we have lots of experience in it. But this can sometimes make us haughty, rendering us susceptible to what is known as "hindsight bias" – after we already know the outcome of an event, we tend to subconsciously recall our original projections incorrectly in a way that makes them match up with what actually ended up happening. It is very difficult to avoid this thinking trap. One first step could be the following: Any time you catch yourself about to say something like "I knew right from the start that…" or "There was obviously no way that could have worked", just pause for a moment and ask yourself whether you might be succumbing to hindsight bias.

4. *The availability heuristic*

People often subconsciously employ the availability heuristic to evaluate situations in which some basic information is lacking – i.e., their decisions in such situations are substantially influenced by whatever information is most quickly and easily available for them to recall. It is irrelevant whether the information is incomplete due to time constraints, disinterest, or actual non-availability – if it is incomplete, we will tend to more readily recall things that were louder, more colorful, or more sensational in some way. For example, we overestimate the probability of being a victim of violence if we have just read a pertinent article in the newspaper – by contrast, however, we generally underestimate the probability of dying from diabetes. In order to cut through this thinking trap, you need to have discourse with "differently minded" people who can contribute their own recollections as well.

5. *Induction*

We infer generalities from individual observations, and arrive at conclusions on the basis of individual pieces of evidence. Here's an example: Mr. Z is an IT professional, and we see that Mr. Z works with the latest technologies. From this, we conclude that all IT professionals are only focused on the latest tools. Evaluating things in such a manner can be dangerous – such as when we incorrectly presume the regularity of some single occurrence even though we could have simply observed further. On the other hand, inductive thinking does offer us a great opportunity to recognize patterns and to extrapolate rules from a series of observations. This is particularly important in managing complex systems; however, it is only valuable if such rules are initially regarded only as hypotheses – and not as absolute truths.

6. *Infallibility*

Experts do not necessarily consider themselves infallible because they are innately too self-assured – rather, they are convinced that they need to be infallible. They are experts in their areas, so they are sought out for advice and need to either make decisions or prepare others for decision-making. Accordingly, they believe that they absolutely cannot make any mistakes. So they analyze things meticulously, consider and reconsider everything, and check all their calculations, until they are "sure". They now believe that they have been so thorough in their work that no mistakes could possibly arise –accordingly, they are infallible. Carefully point out to your experts that they may be subject to one or more thinking traps (to which, incidentally, not only experts are susceptible). Experts are not fundamentally infallible – and this applies both to their field of expertise (in which there may be gaps in their knowledge) and to the ways in which they create their truths (and again, this is not only true of experts).

At the beginning of this chapter, I asked you in what area(s) you are an expert. Since you, too, are an expert, you should reflect upon and perhaps question your own ways of thinking, assessing, and drawing conclusions.

Adaptation versus Exaptation

Many experts are limited to their areas of specialization. They stick to their terrain when searching for solutions, rarely going outside the box. This approach is fostered by the silo mentality that is so prevalent in many organizations. And then there is also our strong need for certainty, which we are most likely to have when experts are thinking and making decisions within their subject areas. So there is a sort of cognitive distortion that leads us to interpret matters as falling within our areas of expertise, even when they do not belong there.

> *"If all you have is a hammer, then every problem will look like a nail."*
> ADAPTED FROM ABRAHAM MASLOW

Now, however, we are faced with the challenge of resolving complex tasks and problems. We want to create new products, to develop our technologies, to make a diverse organization succeed, and to solve global problems. This is not possible with only subject-matter experts. As experts, we tend to remain within our solution spaces and are quite adaptable within these spaces. This means that innovations and solutions are devised on the basis of what is known to us – in other words, an IT guy will solve every problem with IT, an organizational developer will look to the organizational level, and a process consultant will employ new or modified processes. But this is not enough – especially in complex contexts.

 What is needed is a holistic approach that considers all facets of the system in an interdisciplinary manner.

Adaptation (➡ Glossary) does not suffice as a fundamental approach to progress and innovation – especially considering that many significant inventions and achievements have specifically *not* come about as a result of targeted research by experts, but rather have been the result of exaptation (➡ Glossary), which some may also call happenstance or fluke. If adaptation is understood as a function-oriented transformation, then exaptation is the exploitation of an existing function for other purposes. As more and more information becomes available to people, this increases the likelihood of them using some of this information for other purposes, particularly through an interdisciplinary approach. Those who rely on adaptation alone run the risk of getting passed by.

The teabag, for example, was not created intentionally through long and hard deliberations by packaging or tea-brewing experts. During World War I, an American tea trader named Thomas Sullivan put his tea into small silk bags in order to make it easier to provide his customers with small product samples. These customers, however, presumed a different intention behind the bags, and started preparing their tea directly using the bags, thus avoiding having to pour and strain it.

Do you know how the popsicle was invented? One night, when he was eleven years old, Frank Epperson forgot a glass of lemonade outside in the cold with a mixing stick inside it. By the next morning, it had frozen – but it still tasted great. That was in 1905; Epperson patented the idea 18 years later. Likewise, in the 1940s, Percy Spencer was working for a U.S. Defense Department contractor, developing magnetrons for generating radar waves. It was already known at the time that magnetrons produce heat, although this information was not being used for any particular applications. One day, after coming near a magnetron with a chocolate bar in his pocket, Spencer noticed that it had melted – and this chance event gave him the idea for the microwave.

The list could go on and on. The point is that the best solutions and the most innovative ideas are not always generated deliberately through analysis and systematic development processes. Exaptation is not a structured process, but rather a matter of "useful coincidence". We need to keep a broad view in complex contexts – of things to the left and right of our path, of the results of our mistakes, and of ideas outside our areas of expertise. Experts are important to our organizations and projects, and their knowledge is indispensable. At the same time, they represent a special challenge for their managers.

How to properly deal with experts

➢ Experts have invested time and energy in developing their knowledge. Give them the time and space to communicate and apply that knowledge.

➢ Experts want to ensure that their status will be preserved. Do not stoke any unnecessary rivalries in which an expert may lose face.

➢ Experts want recognition – of their expertise and of themselves. Make sure that you give them enough of it.

➢ Experts are constantly looking for greater complexity in their areas. Call upon their expertise in complex tasks.

➢ Experts want to be challenged. Put them up to it.

➢ Experts tend to always regard things as complicated. Put a stop to this, slowly inducing your experts to think "uncomplicatedly" as well.

➢ Experts are sometimes unable to master complex challenges, with analysis being their tool of choice. Never place an expert alone on a complex task.

➢ Support your experts in questioning their perceptions and opening up new perspectives and thought processes.

If expertise cannot be the only approach for dealing with complex challenges in our organizations, then what else do we need? We need generalists, with a variety of skills, perspectives, and ways of thinking. In short – we need diversity (➡ Glossary).

Increase cognitive diversity

Are you familiar with the "Red Team University"? You should be, as it is a fascinating example of successful implementation of the idea of diversity, in an environment that you would not expect – the U.S. Army. Experiences during the chaos of the Iraq war made the military authorities realize something important – that the army needed fewer "yes-men". And this realization brought about a revolution, turning on its head the conventional thinking about how militaries should function.

The Red Team University was founded in 2004 at the Fort Leavenworth army base, under the leadership of Colonel Greg Fontenot. Its objective is to train students as devil's advocates, in order to help commanders avoid falling into typical thinking traps in the theater of operations. Red Team soldiers are trained to question decisions, with the goal of making commanders aware of their own underlying thought patterns and checking their validity. The focus is on aspects such as infallibility, oversimplification, stereotyping, and groupthink.

As expected, the first graduates were initially looked upon with suspicion, and were greeted with hesitation by their colleagues after being deployed. In fact, some of them were actually denied security badges upon their arrival in Baghdad – their colleagues were scared that they might hack into the army's network. Colonel Fontenot described the start of their activities as follows: "What we're really doing is producing an in-house skeptic, and that creates instant antibodies."

The Red Team's approach is never sneaky, however, and its goal is not to search for culprits – quite the contrary. The Red Teamers support commanders in their assessments and decision-making by acting as mirrors and slowing down processes. They challenge opinions, evaluations, and snap judgements in order to facilitate better decisions. We all know, from our own experience, how difficult it is to calmly make good decisions in chaotic, murky situations. When we're right in the middle of it, our view narrows and we draw upon whatever knowledge is quickly and readily available – our familiar patterns, preconceptions, stereotypes, and dogmas. But these things do not necessary constitute the best means for making decisions in our current situation. The job of the Red Team soldiers is to help army commanders broaden their view again.

The training at Fort Leavenworth is hard and intense. Participants in the 18-week program are required to work through around 220 pages of reading per night, occupying themselves with western military theory, counterterrorism, and counterinsurgency. Eastern philosophy and World War II case studies are part of the syllabus, as are negotiation strategies, creative thinking, and behavioral economics. Bob Topping, who developed the program's curriculum, said, "We want them to understand that their view of the world is very narrow. We look at the world through a straw."

This is precisely the understanding that the Red Teamers try to bring to the theater of operations. Everyone behind the program is well aware that this approach runs counter to the prevailing military culture. The Red Teamers have to walk a fine line in their work – they need to assist commanders towards making good decisions, yet without questioning the commanders themselves, which could have fatal consequences for the latter's credibility and authority. If they insist on things too forcefully, there is a risk of no decisions being made at all and the organization simply coming to a standstill. In order to prevent this from happening, Red Teamers must also regularly reflect upon and question their own perspectives and ways of thinking.

The Red Team University is continuing to demonstrate the value of its approach and its work. Even after ten years, there are still reservations – and there will probably continue to be going forward. Even for non-military organizations, this approach is so fascinating because it ensures cognitive diversity – that is, a variety of different perspectives and ways of thinking.

Six good reasons why every organization should have its own "red team":

1. Red teamers help you make good decisions, by looking at complex situations from different perspectives.
2. Red teamers offer tools and methods for questioning one's own perceptions and assessments. They also have relevant background knowledge about theoretical models from different disciplines.
3. Red Teamers assist you in developing alternatives. These may relate to a plan, concept, project, process, or even the organization itself.
4. Red Teamers foster critical and creative thinking.
5. Red Teamers contribute outstanding analytical skills on both the tactical and strategic levels.
6. Red Teamers make us aware of outdated structural and behavioral patterns.

Cognitive diversity increases the number of perspectives, and simultaneously the number of action options. If diversity is allowed on a team, then this results in variety – and this is just what is needed for successfully managing complex tasks. In a complex system, variety can be understood as the number of interrelationships, and thus the degree of complexity. One of the key insights of cybernetics is the Law of Requisite Variety, under which William Ross Ashby explained that a system that regulates another system can compensate for a greater number of disturbances when it itself contains greater variety. This stands to reason – but what does it actually look like in an organization nowadays? Let's first take a look at a prominent example from the past.

On August 26, 1768, Captain James Cook set off for the southern seas aboard the *Endeavour*. His ship had a very diverse 94-man crew: 62 Englishmen, seven Irishmen, nine Scotsmen, five Welshmen, two Africans, three Americans, two Brazilians, a Finn, a Swede, an Italian, and a Tahitian. Eight of them were officers, nine were scientists, and the remaining 77 were sailors. All these different people brought along many different viewpoints with regard to religion and politics.

There are always different views and opinions on any team. One common way of dealing with this diversity is keeping it under wraps. This is not something that necessarily happens with bad intentions, but rather is due to a need for harmony and a desire to achieve goals more quickly. This can backfire, however, with the unaddressed differences constituting a huge potential for conflict. Things that are not discussed openly are nevertheless still there below the surface – and if they are not cleared up in the most sensible places (e.g., meetings), then they just end up surfacing elsewhere.

And so, like-minded people start gossiping over lunch or whispering in the break room, forming their own small groups. In the long run, the absence of an exchange of opinions (and the corresponding lack of understanding of others' perspectives) often leads people to start tactically restricting how they give out information – and the non-transparency that is already inherent in complex situations is now exacerbated even further.

> "It is only through the conflict between opposing opinions that the truth is revealed."
> HELVETIUS

So how should things actually work? Is it just a question of laying all perspectives out on the table, and everything suddenly then becoming easier? Unfortunately, it is not that simple. First, there must be open and respectful interaction, in which each individual learns to tolerate and then value the team's diversity. Of course, the potential for conflict also does manifest itself when differences are addressed – however, the only difference is that now this diversity of opinions is out in the open, instead of simmering below the surface. The essential point here is that only with an open approach to diversity can all participants learn. Resources can only be utilized and developed (with regard to both the individual and the team) via discourse. And the basis for this is trust. In order to create a good foundation for diversity, you should make the following elements take root in your team:

- ➤ *Openness:*
  - – *An appetite for other perspectives and experiences*
  - – *A readiness to hear other opinions*
  - – *A willingness to take others seriously*
- ➤ *Invitation:*
  - – *New colleagues are welcome*
  - – *A desire to learn the new colleagues' perspectives*
- ➤ *Appreciation:*
  - – *A focus on shared values*
  - – *Respect and tolerance for other people*
- ➤ *Understanding:*
  - – *Reflection upon one's own thinking and behavior*
- ➤ *Self-perception:*
  - – *An awareness of diversity*
- ➤ *Communication:*
  - – *Awareness of speech patterns (terminology, etc.) used in the team*
- ➤ *Individuality instead of adaptation:*
  - – *Avoidance of groupthink*
- ➤ *Discourse is welcome*
  - – *A desire for debate within the team*

SUMMING UP:

- ❖ We are trained and educated as experts.
- ❖ Experts are at home when dealing with complicated problems.
- ❖ Complicated problems are linear and can be solved through analysis.
- ❖ Complex tasks, however, require a variety of opinions, perspectives, and ideas.
- ❖ Real diversity requires trust and openness.

Misconception #4:
We can't afford to make
any mistakes

Allow me to introduce you to Malu Dreyer, the first woman to serve as Minister-President of the German state of Rhineland-Palatinate. Dreyer, a lawyer, succeeded Kurt Beck in 2013, after serving for several years in Beck's cabinet as State Minister of Social Affairs, Labor, Health, and Demography. In the autumn of 2013, she suddenly became a much more public figure than she probably would have liked, as her name was splashed all over the major German newspapers and magazines, including, of course, the tabloids.

What happened? Ms. Dreyer had written a letter to German chancellor Angela Merkel on September 6, 2013, requesting a top-level meeting between the federal and state governments regarding the NSA scandal. But the news here was not in the contents of her letter, but rather in the errors it contained. Yes, that's right – Ms. Dreyer made spelling and grammar mistakes in a letter to the country's chancellor. The Bild tabloid counted six errors in six sentences. Spiegel Online counted eight.

In any case, it was a big scandal – so big that Die Welt published a copy of the letter with the errors marked in red, annotated schoolteacher-style in the margin. Ms. Dreyer was then showered with derision, accusations of incompetence, and guilt. Her staff, of course, was guilty alongside her. The press asked lots of questions: Who signs off on such letters? How could this happen? Whose fault was it? How embarrassing could such a thing be? But the question on my mind was: Whew, can we all just tone it down a notch?

Letters should obviously be written correctly, no matter to whom they are addressed. It would be great if they always were. But honestly, this incident is actually just a threadlike reflection of our general attitude towards mistakes. Mistakes are not allowed – not in what we write, not in what we do, not in what we say, and not in the decisions we make. When we discover other people's errors, our teacher instinct immediately kicks in – we pull out our red pens and comment, "Wrong!" This is the only way that I can explain how Malu Dreyer's letter was published in *Die Welt*. After all, we learn at school that mistakes are bad, and that we are only doing well if we don't get things wrong. This is deeply ingrained in us for life.

Did you ever have a teacher return an assignment so covered in red that you could barely even read what you had originally written anymore? I, personally, looked for patterns in the red markings. And did you ever make a mistake when called up to the blackboard, causing all your classmates to break out in laughter? Or perhaps you had to show your parents a report card with "unsatisfactory" marks, eliciting that disappointed look on their faces. And so on and so forth...

"That's wrong." "That's not right." "You're wrong." "You're not right." Can you still hear in your head that voice that has been pointing out mistakes since our school days? That was a long time ago, of course, but "Don't make any mistakes!" is still deeply ingrained inside us – and still affects our behavior. Because school was just the beginning; the same attitude towards errors exists at our universities and in our companies. Errors are undesirable, they are not tolerated, and they will be punished.

The "classic" way of dealing with errors, as manifested during our adult lives, can be observed particularly well in the political arena. And this is true with regard to both the person who makes a mistake and those who react to the mistake. Two sides of the same coin – and it has a lot to do with morality.

On February 18, 2011, German Minister of Defense Karl-Theodor zu Guttenberg made a statement before a group of journalists, during which the otherwise-quite-eloquent politician gave off a very uneasy image as he tried to explain to the media that his dissertation was not, in fact, plagiarized. He avoided looking at the cameras or the journalists when he talked about deception, copying, or himself. He looked down at the floor instead.

Although the dissertation contained errors, he said, he himself had not made any. And even throughout the various sessions that followed at the German Bundestag, he never said, "I've made a mistake" or "I've done something wrong." Instead, he switched to an impersonal general pronoun whenever he spoke about himself, creating a sort of distance between himself and the words he was saying. He fought so hard not to admit to any mistakes, leaving the impression that he would be ashamed. Meanwhile, we, the viewers, were thinking, "He certainly *should* be ashamed."

One could almost feel sorry for him – but I really just wanted to yell, "Stop it, just talk straight with us!" However, admitting to having made a mistake here would have constituted acknowledgement that he had committed a fraud, so Guttenberg just stuck to his claim that he had neither consciously nor intentionally made any mistake. He eventually resigned, accompanied by lots of ill will and wagging fingers. We were all outraged: "It's unacceptable! Other people work so hard, and then this snotty aristocrat just goes and..." Even Annette Schavan, the Minister for Education and Research at the time, quite openly expressed how ashamed she was of Guttenberg – and then, two years later, she faced the very same allegations with regard to her own doctoral thesis.

We have seen such scenes play out in every political scandal both before and since Guttenberg's, with different protagonists each time. And what do we learn from them? If you make a mistake, here is what you do: Express outrage, deny, distract people if possible, divert their attention elsewhere, and only then admit to the error and accept the consequences. In short: Don't let them catch you! So we try to avoid making mistakes, or at least admitting to them. It's what we've learned to do in school, and it's what we continue to see every day in the worlds of politics and business – so, it's what we do ourselves. We all demand politicians and business leaders who are honest and authentic, but woe is to those who actually are!

Why we are afraid of mistakes

A mistake is made – and immediately, the search for the responsible party begins. The first question is usually, "How could this have happened?" And then, we ask ourselves how we can avoid such errors in the future. It doesn't matter what kind of error happened – a product that doesn't work right, a coworker who didn't relay information in time, a technical system with a bug, or a project that fell behind schedule. When we find out who is responsible for the mistake, an appropriate penalty is immediately imposed. This presumably puts things back in order. Everyone calms down – even the person responsible, who hangs his head in shame and vows to himself that he will be more careful next time.

It's like a reflex – naming, blaming, shaming. The blame for mistakes, errors, and irregularities is almost always assigned to an individual – and this person is categorized as the "guilty" one, who should be ashamed of what he did. For everyone else, this perspective is not only practical, in the sense of them being categorized as "not guilty", but it also simple and linear. It gives us all a sense of certainty when we know that the reason, cause, and perpetrator of the mistake can be identified quickly and unambiguously. However, it is a false sense of certainty, as we ourselves are now making a mistake – the "there's always a linear causal relationship" mistake.

But why don't we just escape the naming-blaming-shaming game? Since childhood, we have been taught that those who make mistakes are not accepted. Rather, they are spurned, cast out, and punished for their behavior and actions. Many people are willing to expend lots of energy to make sure that they don't experience such rejection (again). They avoid making mistakes, whenever and wherever possible. One of our basic needs is the need for recognition and acceptance – being shunned is one of the worst possible punishments. In our day-to-day working lives, this often means that we would rather work through our tasks strictly "by the book" than run the risk of making an error.

> *"I've missed more than 9,000 shots in my career. I've lost almost 300 games. 26 times, I've been trusted to take the game-winning shot and missed. I've failed over and over and over again in my life. And that is why I succeed."*
> MICHAEL JORDAN

This quote from Michael Jordan shows a very high degree of self-awareness. An athlete of this level certainly has a strong sense of self-esteem. He knows for what portion of his successes and failures he is responsible himself. He is well aware that, in his area of expertise, mistakes are inevitable. After all, he is not a machine, and basketball is a complex game. Most people can easily understand his perspective.

But what about in the context of managing an organization? What about when the goal is a certain level of market penetration or sales volume, or the development of a new product, or the restructuring of a company? Does the "success-through-failure" approach still apply? You may be thinking that these situations are completely different from Michael Jordan's. But management is just as complex a task as basketball. In order to be successful in complex contexts, we need to test out different procedures, processes, materials, responses, etc. – and this will inevitably bring about errors (i.e., unwanted reactions and results).

But we are afraid of this, and so we follow certain specific behavioral patterns. On the personal level, we protect our own self-esteem by simply avoiding mistakes and errors – and by not admitting to those that we do make. This phenomenon is quite prevalent in our organizations. We prefer to deny mistakes rather than admit to them, because we are afraid of being put to shame, of the feeling of being wrong, and of the social penalties that we may suffer as a result. The manner in which mistakes are handled forms part of a company's culture – and it is among the unwritten rules that we learn rather quickly.

A company's culture shapes how it deals with errors

There is great ambivalence in our organizational cultures with regard to errors. On one hand, our company guidelines always say things like "We deal with errors openly and constructively" or "We learn from our mistakes." But on the other hand, in reality, those who do err often find themselves pilloried. Each person's attitude towards slip-ups and his manner of dealing with them are shaped by two things: the company's culture and the individual's socialization with regard to mistakes.

Honestly – what attitude do you and your organization have when it comes to dealing with mistakes?

	Yes	No
We actively learn from our mistakes.		
I take responsibility for my team's mistakes, even to my superiors.		
When a mistake is made, we focus on the resulting damage.		
We concentrate on finding the guilty party.		
We focus on avoiding such mistakes in the future.		
Employees who openly admit to their mistakes are accepted for it.		
I, personally, admit to my mistakes, instead of foisting responsibility for them upon others.		
Errors are important feedback that fosters development.		
Learning from mistakes is better than simply standing still without making any mistakes.		

The attitude that "We can't afford to make mistakes" is not only obstructive in complex contexts – it is actually a serious hindrance to success. Remember, when dealing with complex situations or problems, classical analysis is not what leads us to decisions – rather, the tools of choice are testing and experimentation. In a system whose future states of affairs are unpredictable, a manager can give impulses to stimulate certain behavior. This is what testing is about. The behavior that results is then assessed. If the behavior is desirable, then it can be reinforced; if it is undesirable, then the manager can intervene accordingly. This is reacting, i.e., decision-making. In many situations, the decision-making process is already taking place in this manner even without us being aware of it.

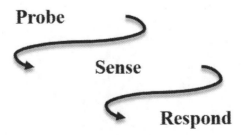

Probing instead of analyzing leads to good decisions.

We need to make errors – because if we do not, then we will never master complexity.

A good example of testing as a basis for decision-making is team-building. When there are departmental changes in a company, team-building events are often organized by the management, with the goal of enabling coworkers to get to know each other better and developing or strengthening a sense of unity. Possible activities range from raft-building to go-karting to team cooking. Only in retrospect is it possible to say whether the event has had the desired effect on the fabric of the team – this is not possible a priori. No one can preordain a causal relationship between the event and the team's behavior or thinking.

Companies, however, often see things differently, demanding that the moderator/consultant/coach to do whatever it takes to make the team think or do X, Y, and Z. People are sometimes susceptible to the mistaken belief that one person can determine another's way of thinking – however, this is not something that anyone can promise to do, at least not seriously. Mental models and behavioral patterns only start manifesting themselves during and after the team-building event. If these patterns match what the company was seeking – lucky them. If not, then they just blame the moderator/consultant/ coach. An unsuitable moderator matched with an unsuitable event theme and an unsuitable team can obviously be held partly responsible for the failure of a team-building event, but only partly. What is more sensible at this point, though, is to consciously abandon the blame game and instead work with the team's observable behavioral and communication patterns. Give stimuli, observe, evaluate the patterns that emerge, and then react accordingly. This is what mastering complexity is about. You will repeatedly find yourself at points in which undesirable patterns will emerge and errors will reveal themselves.

The changes, problems, and challenges that you face are highly complex. Maybe the last quarter was bad, or there's been a change on the board of directors, or your biggest competitor caught everyone off guard with a great new product. Why anything has happened precisely as it happened is something that we can only discern in retrospect.

There are two essential qualities that you must have as a manager – courage and patience.

To master complexity, master courage and patience.

You need courage to choose and initiate the necessary experiments – and patience to wait for patterns to emerge before you make decisions and react. The main sticking point in many organizations is that experiments are chosen when "success is guaranteed". These organizations try to solve complex problems in a linear and fail-safe manner. But rather than being fail-safe, experiments geared towards solving complex problems must instead follow the "safe-fail" principle.

Fail-safe or safe-fail – a question of culture

Every organization lies somewhere on the spectrum between fail-safe (➡ Glossary) and safe-fail (➡ Glossary). It comes down to the difference between damage avoidance and damage mitigation. Organizations and systems that prefer the fail-safe approach try to safeguard themselves against any failures, using spare parts, redundancies, and double windows. We thus impute to them a certain immunity to errors, as we get lulled into a (supposed) sense of security.

The safe-fail approach, on the other hand, is based on the assumption that failures and errors will happen and that this is unavoidable. With errors being presumed, the focus is on preserving the purpose, goals, and structure of the system despite these errors. In my experience, most organizations try to be as fail-safe as possible – believing that nothing should go wrong and that no mistakes at all should be made. Zero-tolerance is the goal, regardless of whether we are talking about standardized production processes or project management. The idea is to make sure the system is so robust, foolproof, and braced for any eventualities that nothing can go wrong anymore. Every effort is made to radically reduce the possibility of errors, mistakes, or failures, and the managers end up behaving as if this possibility were truly zero.

Good examples of this include nuclear power plants and aircraft production. Every nuclear power plant has a fail-safe emergency backup for the power supply. In the event of a power failure, hydraulics ensure that the backup power supply takes over and injects the control rods into the reactor. The system thus remains safe. Well, that's what the people in charge of the Fukushima nuclear power plant thought too. And after the March 11, 2011 earthquake had incapacitated the main power supply, the emergency system initially did take over. So far, everything was going according to the fail-safe plan. But the tsunami that followed then brought the backup system to its knees as well. The cooling failed, and the rest is history. The question arose, of course, as to why there was no third-level backup mechanism in place. The answer was that the probability of being struck by an earthquake and a tsunami in such quick succession was extremely low.

And therein lies the faulty thinking: We think linearly and base our actions upon the probabilities of specific potential errors, instead of anticipating how we might handle all different future scenarios without lurching into catastrophes or problems. We spend too much time and energy thinking about what particular things could go wrong in the future and about what specific steps we can take in response – meanwhile, we ignore the fact that the future could end up being entirely different than anything we have considered. When it comes to designing systems, we still see robustness and an immunity to errors as essential features. But in the long run, this leads to any eventual mistakes being even more costly, as they end up having more serious consequences and being more expensive to fix.

At the same time, an organization that has such a policy with regard to errors is continuously paying a fee in terms of flexibility and adaptability. The reduced adaptability is because the organization puts all of its efforts into preparing for the most expected disturbances to the system – so in the event of an unforeseen occurrence, the system gets severely disturbed and thrown completely off course. A highly adaptable system, by contrast, is set up in a way that takes into account the fact that there may always be disturbances and events that cannot be identified in advance – and thus, it is highly capable of adapting to the unknown. This adaptability arises particularly as a result of a corresponding inner attitude on the part of the people involved. It is only in the next step that measures and precautions then emerge.

 Adaptive systems (⇒ Glossary) survive "no matter what happens".

The safe-fail principle assumes that mistakes and failures will always happen. In a complex environment, in which new solutions and innovations are important, searching for the single right solution is a pure waste of time – too many linear attempts are needed in order to eventually find a suitable solution. Experience and an idea of what a solution might look like are the inputs that we use when testing – and this approach will always produce errors. Additionally, a complex system cannot be designed or customized according to specifications; we can only stimulate it in order to cause patterns to emerge, allowing us to recognize the evolutionary possibilities. This stimulation should happen via many parallel safe-fail experiments that enable us to look at a problem or topic from different angles. These experiments should each be small and limited – so the costs in the event of failure are limited accordingly, and the system thus does not falter. Complexity demands a higher tolerance for errors in an organization; this is the only way that it will manage to remain adaptable.

"Safe-fail" does not mean minimizing errors, but rather keeping the costs of any errors low.

Errors are not only tolerated and accepted – rather, errors (or conflicts that lead to errors) are made to happen in a controlled manner. Canadian ecologist Buzz Holling, in his publication "Fail-Safe vs. Safe-Fail Catastrophes" (Holling / Jones / Peterman, 1975), demonstrates this principle through a ritual that exists among one population group in New Guinea, serving to regulate their system. This group mainly obtains its food from the surrounding forests and from their gardens. The consumption of pork is important to them, but it may only be eaten on certain ceremonial occasions. These ceremonies happen whenever the "social temperature" among the population reaches a certain point where conflicts arise – pigs are then slaughtered and eaten, and this serves to appease the gods.

The main reason for the conflicts that arise is the high pig population itself. The many pigs eventually start ravaging gardens, making troubles between neighbors inevitable. After the festive ceremony, however, these problems are magically resolved. The ritual is not really geared towards keeping the pig population under control – it is rather a matter of this society protecting itself from uncontrolled instability as a result of conflicts.

> "Human beings, who are almost unique in having the ability to learn from the experience of others, are also remarkable for their apparent disinclination to do so."
> DOUGLAS ADAMS

If this particular society were fail-safe, there would probably be guidelines regulating the maximum number of pigs per household or per village. This would give them a perceived certainty that no conflicts could arise between people as a result of the pigs. Individuals and the community would have less freedom with regard to pig farming. There might still be some sort of ceremonies, although these would happen at fixed times and basically for no concrete reason.

Instead of minimizing the probability of problems occurring, this population group has found a method for generating controlled failures. The ravaged gardens and resulting conflicts between neighbors are clear signals that the system is in need of a correction. And so, the ceremony is performed. It decimates the pig population and provides an opportunity to resolve conflicts. The system is self-organized, instead of being over regulated; there are just a few restrictions that provide for the regulation of the system. The sort of instability that manifests itself through the rising "social temperature" is something that occurs on a regular basis and preserves the flexibility of the society. Meanwhile, it also ensures the necessary resolution of conflicts.

An organization's "error culture" (i.e., its attitude towards errors) determines how easy or difficult it may be for you to set up and carry out safe-fail experiments. And these sorts of experiments are precisely what you need in order to adequately solve complex problems.

 It takes too much time to follow the "trial and error" method of linearly working through the trials with the highest probability of success. Solving complex problems requires many iterations in short intervals.

If you do not produce any errors and you never fail, then you will not exhaust all possibilities to learn about your context. Remember: errors are understood as undesirable results (or patterns) – we must be able to go back from the point of an undesired result to correct it.

In software development, for example, this means discarding the approach of "specification of requirements – software design – coding – testing – approval". All too often, the end of this process comes with a realization that what was developed was not exactly what the client wanted. Software development in small modules, with discussions and corrections handled together with the client throughout the development process, is more effective. Correcting the software "along the way" is much easier and cheaper. It is no wonder that the concept of agile software development has been gaining popularity in recent years – but more on this later.

Basic principles for safe-fail experiments:

1. *Carry out small, meaningful experiments.*
   The goal of experimenting is to allow patterns to emerge. This requires considering tasks or problems from different angles.

2. *Expect and produce errors.*
   Errors are a feedback for the system; they facilitate the learning process.

3. *Carry out different experiments in the same context.*
   Different experiments give rise to variety (i.e., different action or communication options).

4. *Carry out the same experiment in different contexts.*
   A single experiment could have completely different results in different contexts.

5. *Set clear definitions for the success or failure of an experiment.*
   There must be clear decision-making criteria in order to guide the way forward.

6. *Carry out experiments in parallel, not sequentially.*
   Modular, delimited experiments should be going on simultaneously, in order to avoid time delays. When a failed experiment is ended, another experiment should be initiated right away.

Google – The master of safe-fail experiments

Are you familiar with a location-based social networking service Dodgeball? Or does the name Jaiku ring a bell? What about the collaboration platform Wave? Google Catalogs? The CR48 notebook? Mashup Editor? No? Well, it doesn't matter, because all of these services and products were failed experiments. And all by Google – a company that is known for its success, and by now for its management as well. In addition to many of the company's noteworthy structural aspects, it is an ability to make mistakes and learn from them that lies behind Google's success. Projects are terminated as soon as they are deemed unsuccessful; failure is an essential part of the company's plan for success. Terminating a product or project also means freeing up resources – including intellectual, temporal, and financial resources.

For many years, Google has given its approximately 20,000 employees free time for experimentation. For about 20 percent of each employee's working time, they can and should be "engineers" – developing, building, and testing out innovations. Many potential products have been designed in this manner. Ideas that caught on within the company have been tested in the market. Often, they were still in the beta stage and thus unfinished products. Needless to say, not everything that has been conceptualized and designed in this manner could be successful. What is Google's approach? Rather than looking at the risks involved in individual projects and following a classical risk management schema in which the costs of failures are the decisive factors, the company has carried out lots of manageable, modular experiments that individually have posed no risk to the company's overall success. Twitter is another illustration of this, with even users playing a role in shaping the service – it was the users who brought the famous hashtag symbol to the website, not the other way around.

A Google-style attitude towards errors can be summarized as follows:

➢ Test many things out.
➢ Assume that some of them will fail.
➢ Limit the costs of potential failures.
➢ Admit to mistakes and failures at an early stage.

"We celebrate our failures."
ERIC SCHMIDT, FORMER GOOGLE CEO

Dealing with errors meaningfully

We are currently living in a performance-oriented society, in which we are measured by our successes and condemned for our failures. Even though the concept of failure has found its way into management literature, expectations for one's own performance (and non-failure) are still very high. Business psychologist Michael Frese has extensively studied how errors are dealt with in different countries. Germany performs poorly in his study, coming in next-to-last place out of 61 countries analyzed.

Culture shapes how people think and act in every country, organization, and team. Does a new way of dealing with errors automatically mean that the culture will change as well? Yes, in the long run. In my discussions with managers, I often hear the argument that changing a culture is a tedious, difficult, and rarely successful endeavor. And I have also encountered the opposite – the "okay, we'll change our culture right away" attitude. Cultures develop – they are not simply "made". They are the sum of all the values, norms, and rules in a system. If we change our mindsets, perspectives, or behaviors, then the culture will also change in the long run. There is thus no convincing argument here against adopting a different approach to dealing with mistakes and failures.

For success in complex situations and in dealing with complex problems, the following should be considered and implemented:

> *"I ~~am~~ made a mistake."*
  Thomas Alva Edison once said, "I have not failed. I've just found ten thousand ways that won't work." Be like Edison – and see your mistakes and failures as learning opportunities. Separate how you judge the (undesired) result from how you judge yourself.

> *Errors are feedback for the system*
  When errors are made, do not only look backwards to identify guilty parties. Instead, ask yourself, "What does this error say about the system as a whole, and what does it mean for our future actions?"

> *Errors make us wiser*
  Create an environment in your organization that allows everyone to learn from any errors that are made. In order for employees to be able to admit to mistakes, the working relationship must be based on trust. Take the lead as a manager – and offer trust instead of just demanding it.

> *"There's always something."*
  In a complex, dynamic environment, it is impossible to have 100% perfection. With a mantra of "expect the unexpected", you can accept the uncertainty and non-transparency that are inherent in the system.

> *"Just barely got it right."*
  Take advantage of near-failures as clues regarding possible weaknesses in your system, rather than simply seeing them as proof of your invulnerability.

> *Keep an eye out*
  Train yourself to pay attention to early signals and hints. Mistakes and turmoil do foreshadow themselves – so be alert.

> *The proof of the pudding…*
  Use safe-fail experiments for solving complex problems – and remember that some of them must fail in order for you to make full use of your scope for learning.

➤ *Put a stop to the blame game*

End the blame game in your organization, and encourage your employees to admit to their mistakes. Discuss the effects, consequences, and implications of such errors, rather than the guilty parties.

➤ *Learning through repetition*

Can you only make an error once? No, you can (and sometimes should) make it several times – the implications may be completely different in a different context.

➤ *Don't fall into the causality trap*

Be careful not to be a victim of the causality trap, seeing errors in a purely linear, cause-and-effect way. Think in terms of reciprocal relationships.

SUMMING UP:

- ❖ We must make errors if we want to master complexity.
- ❖ Errors constitute essential feedback.
- ❖ We need safe-fail experiments, instead of fail-safe endeavors.
- ❖ Trial-and-error is linear and takes too long.
- ❖ A company's attitude towards errors affects its employees' thinking and actions.
- ❖ It takes courage to make mistakes.
- ❖ Experimentation requires patience – patterns usually do not emerge ad hoc.

Misconception #5: Good planning is everything

"Those who travel have stories to tell," wrote Matthias Claudius. It all starts, of course, with how they plan their travels – and I personally know some unique specimens when it comes to travel planning! A good acquaintance of mine who travels frequently – let's call him Konrad – figures he spends about eight times as much time planning each journey as he does on the journey itself. And he certainly does not lack experience, having already travelled to every continent.

The process is always the same. He books his trip at least a year in advance, and then buys and studies all of the main travel guides for his destination. Now he knows what sights are on his must-see list, as well as what kind of weather he should expect during mornings, afternoons, and evenings on his trip. Several weeks before his departure, Konrad prepares an essential packing list that just keeps growing, from A for anti-dandruff shampoo to Z for ziploc bags – he doesn't want to forget anything important. Needless to say, he has nametags sewn into all of his jackets and coats, since they are sometimes hung out of his sight at restaurants and one never knows what might happen...

As the day of his departure approaches, Konrad starts checking his planned taxi, rail, and flight connections on a daily basis – after all, there could always be a railway strike or a change in the flight schedule. If maintenance is being done on the railway line, he calculates an appropriate time buffer and discusses the matter in detail with the railways hotline. It once got to the point where the railway company actually had to promise Konrad that they would get him to the airport on time. On time, in Konrad's case, means three-and-a-half hours before the flight – he would rather have an extra coffee at the airport than risk missing his flight (which, incidentally, has never happened). Recently, he had ordered a taxi to bring him to the airport at 3:30 A.M. – but after a colleague told him that she had once (!) had to wait for such a taxi in the middle of the night, Konrad called up the taxi dispatcher and changed it 3 o'clock instead. Just to be sure.

His suitcase is well packed, double-secured against bursting open, and marked in an easily recognizable manner – because everyone's suitcases seem to look the same nowadays. He has also weighed it at least four times before leaving, in order to make sure that it falls within the airline's weight limits.

After checking in his luggage, Konrad can relax until the boarding call. He then boards the plane, takes his seat (always an aisle seat for the legroom), and soon is finally airborne – and if all goes according to plan, he will enjoy a splendid vacation. He knows exactly what he wants to see and do during each and every day of his trip. Everything has been carefully thought out and meticulously planned.

And then, the unthinkable happens: Konrad's luggage does not arrive at his destination. It has disappeared. The worst possible disaster has come to pass. But everything was prepared so carefully! How could this have happened? What is he supposed to do now? Everything that he needs is inside his suitcase – how is he going to get it back now? Questions, questions, and more questions, as Konrad grows more and more upset.

His vacation is done – there is no way that he will be able to relax now. Konrad is so intensely preoccupied with the fact that he doesn't have his luggage that he is unable to think about anything else besides getting it back, no matter the cost. After two days, many telephone calls, and countless visits to the hotel reception desk, he finally gets his suitcase back. Everything is still there. But still, he simply cannot relax properly anymore. None of this should have happened – everything had been planned out so well...

Planning comes before action

Regardless of whether it's a vacation, a major project, the development of a software application, the upcoming financial quarter, or the launch of a new product – we always want to be sure that anything important, difficult, or complicated has been carefully thought through and systematically planned out. It gives us a sense of certainty, preserving the illusion that it is possible to predict our results and the future.

Don't get me wrong – planning is fundamentally a good thing. We should differentiate, however, between where planning is meaningful and where it no longer is – and we need to be aware of how complexity affects our ability to plan things. The more unclear or turbulent the situation, the more closely we often plan; however, the more unclear or turbulent the situation, the worse our planning often is. This is not arbitrary and it is not intentional – rather, it is tied to the question of how individuals deal with complex situations.

Psychologist Dietrich Dörner has carried out many fascinating experiments in precisely this regard, as described in his book *The Logic of Failure* (1996). I have selected one experiment to sketch out here briefly, in order to illustrate some essential facets of planning and complexity. The experiment involved a computer simulation in which 48 different participants were allowed to control the fate of a fictional town named Greenvale. The participants could exercise almost dictatorial powers over the town for a period of ten years, and they could not be voted out of office or anything of the sort. It was thought that giving them as much freedom and power as possible would serve as a breeding ground for success.

> *"In planning we don't do anything; we just consider what we might do."*
> DIETRICH DÖRNER

Greenvale has a population of around 3,700. Its economic focal point is the municipal watch factory, where most local residents work, and it has a fairly average infrastructure. Key parameters such as the town's revenues, its unemployment rate, the watch factory's production levels, the number of people looking for housing, and the inhabitants' general satisfaction were calculated and tracked for each mayor (i.e., experiment participant) over the course of the simulation. Dörner and his team were particularly interested in extracting information regarding the thinking and planning strategies of the participants, as well as how they hypothesized. Significant strategic differences became apparent between the so-called "good" mayors and "bad" mayors, a distinction that was made on the basis of the aforementioned key parameters.

"Good" mayors

- ➢ *made more decisions*
- ➢ *found more ways to influence the town's fate*
- ➢ *thought through their decisions systematically, taking interrelationships into account*
- ➢ *found more alternatives per goal*
- ➢ *tested and questioned their hypotheses*
- ➢ *inquired about many causal relationships*
- ➢ *focused on the relevant topic in their discussions and while developing solutions*

"Bad" mayors

- ➢ *made fewer decisions*
- ➢ *focused on individual aspects and outcomes in an isolated manner*
- ➢ *instead of hypotheses, produced subjective truths without further examination*
- ➢ *took events as given*
- ➢ *jumped back and forth between different topics in their discussions*
- ➢ *got diverted to harmless topics instead of striking the iron that was hot*

Regarding planning, the conclusions were as follows: The "good" mayors found the right/important action areas, and then stayed on the ball. The "bad" mayors, on the other hand, tended towards what Dörner called "repair service behavior". For example, one mayor calculated the average distance that the average senior citizen had to walk to a phone booth in Greenvale, and used this as a basis for placing new telephone booths in the town – he preferred to solve a problem that he *could* solve, rather than focus on the problems that he *should* solve. "Bad" mayors also preferred to deal with a variety of issues quickly and superficially, rather than devote sufficient time to dealing with the truly important issues. It becomes clear at this point that whether one was a "good" mayor or a "bad" mayor had nothing at all to do with the person's intelligence – there were other things behind it.

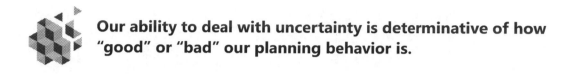 **Our ability to deal with uncertainty is determinative of how "good" or "bad" our planning behavior is.**

Uncertainty leads to more planning... and more planning leads to more uncertainty

When we cannot fully grasp situations or problems, we tend towards more precise and meticulous planning. We feel like we must identify every possibility and take into account everything that could potentially happen. Unfortunately, this often leads to an increase in our own uncertainty, as the amount of information and scenarios just continues to grow. The situation now seems even farther outside our grasp. And yet we still tend to continue with more of the same, planning in even greater detail and thus maneuvering ourselves even deeper into the complexity trap.

We fall into this trap without realizing it due to a sort of positive feedback that exists inside us as a system. Uncertainty makes us obtain more information, this additional information makes us uncertain as well, which makes us obtain even more information, and so on. This feedback cycle escalates until either we have gathered "enough" information or we simply terminate the cycle because we have reached our limit. Terminating the cycle either results in a dead-end – nothing decided, nothing done, the plan tossed out, the project abandoned – or makes us lapse into just taking action blindly. The complexity trap thus makes us act rashly, declaring it as "intuition" even though what we are basically doing is just taking action for the sake of taking action. Quality suffers from this, along with everyone involved.

How do you deal with such non-transparent planning situations? What "strategies" do you use? You may recognize your approach in the following list:

> **Evasive maneuvers used in complex planning situations:**
>
> ➤ *Distraction*: When planning and decision-making become difficult in complex situations, you direct your attention to others (coworkers, other departments, suppliers), who are supposed to do or decide or deliver something. Or you divert your focus to issues and problems that lie completely outside your current decision space.
>
> ➤ *Encapsulation*: In order to escape the feeling of uncertainty (at least for a while), you focus on a single detail that you can plan and process well. This gives you a sense of certainty – while also protecting you from having to make tougher decisions and take action.
>
> ➤ *Baby steps*: You plan in smaller steps with greater detail, putatively to give yourself a better view of the big picture. This gives you a sense of certainty, but you run the risk of oversimplifying everything because complexity cannot be made linear just by breaking it down into smaller parts.
>
> ➤ *Focus on formal methodology*: This is another common sort of distraction maneuver that is supposed to give you a sense of certainty. If you follow a specific method, then your planning must be good, right? There is again, however, a risk of oversimplification.
>
> ➤ *"The way we've always done it"*: At first glance, making recourse to a proven blueprint seems like a recipe for success. But take a second glance – because such blueprints were usually used in other contexts and are not necessarily suitable for the situation at hand. The sense of certainty that they give you may end up being short-lived.

So uncertainty is a key factor that can hamper our planning and often ultimately results in us not making decisions or taking action. However, uncertainty is not the only reason that projects and companies fail. There are yet other pitfalls that one may encounter when planning under conditions of complexity.

The plan was good – but it didn't work out

In many cases where large public projects have been declared disasters by the media, there have been those who predicted already in the planning phase that the project would go wrong – and there turned out to be truth in those predictions. Planning is an important cornerstone that is laid upon a base of assumptions, hypotheses, goals, and interests – and when there is much diversity among them, it creates a marvelous breeding ground for planning catastrophes. Here is a recent example.

By the time the JadeWeserPort, Germany's only deep-water port, opened in September 2012, almost no one believed anymore that it would be successful. However, the port had everything that it needed to be a success: an area of about 500 football fields, its own highway exit, a 16-track railway installation, eight huge container cranes, and 1.7 kilometers of harbor quays. The German states of Lower Saxony and Bremen had ambitious goals and promised that the facility would create many jobs. The JadeWeserPort was to be the third-largest international port in Germany, with a capacity of 2.7 million containers shipped per year. Around 390 hectares of sand were extracted so that the harbor could handle even the largest container ships, such as the Maersk E-class. The port was built as a new district of the town of Wilhelmshaven, and it was forecasted that the port operations alone would create 1,000 new jobs, with shipping companies, warehousing, and railway services creating 1,000 more. The harbor was to give new life to Germany's less-developed northwestern corner; Wilhelmshaven and its surrounding region could contribute very little in this regard, due to the limited commercial activity in the area.

The results after two years of operations? A financial disaster, with little prospect of improvement. Only about two ships dock in the harbor per week. And most of them don't have much cargo to process there – they are just using Wilhelmshaven as a stopover. Fewer than 64,000 containers were handled in the port's first year. Already in 2013, almost all of the employees of operating partner Eurogate were put on short-time work, a situation that still had not changed by the end of 2014. Meanwhile, the Nordfrost company complained to the port operator about the fact that it had invested millions there in the expansion of its fruit and vegetable business – but the lack of ships has meant that its cold storage facilities have been lying empty and no revenue has been coming in.

Already in its first year of operations, the JadeWeserPort fell far behind the 700,000 containers that it had promised to handle that year – however, in spite of this, the further expansion of the port is still not yet off the table. The plan calls for more berths; it makes reference to the large Triple-E-class container ships. The shipping companies do not see the need for this, as they can just head for the ports of Hamburg or Bremerhaven. Even Maersk, the second active operator, sees no need for expansion – quite to the contrary, its main business is still running through the other two ports.

Environmentalists, of course, have been up in arms about the construction of this huge facility. Two beaches were destroyed in the process, and rare shorebirds have had their breeding areas threatened. Long-term effects on nature, however, have had no effect on the considerations of the parties involved in the project. Cracks in the sheet piling intermittently delayed the project and had to be repaired at great cost. There were also no (published) examinations of the long-term effects of the massive interference with flow conditions in the Jade Bight. What has long been clear, however, is that tourism in Wilhelmshaven is suffering due to the loss of the two beaches as well as a portion of the local camping area.

So, there you have some basic information about the JadeWeserPort. With regard to planning, it is most interesting to look at the project's underlying forecasts and hypotheses. On what basis was the port planned and built? In 1993, when the project was launched, economic projections said that container traffic would continue to rise by 6% per year until 2025. This was before the economic crisis, however. So the simplistic assessment of the situation went as follows: A deep-water port is needed, Wilhelmshaven needs a spark, so let's build it there.

The information detailed above raises some questions. A look around reveals many factors that should have been taken into account – were these contexts not even considered, or were they simply blocked out because they didn't match the starry-eyed forecast for the JadeWeserPort? To start, Rotterdam was already planning an expansion of its port – which has been completed in the meantime, and surpasses Wilhelmshaven's by a factor of five. A new container port was planned in London as well. Also, Maersk was operating at full capacity in Hamburg and Bremerhaven, and moving its business to Wilhelmshaven would have resulted in losses. This situation has not changed. In Hamburg, the project to deepen of the Elbe River is also seen as essential for protecting jobs in the region.

Given all this, what was the eventual conclusion of the responsible parties? That the JadeWeserPort was unfortunately launched at the wrong time, but will end up being necessary in the long run.

Plans – Little helpers or steel corsets?

The example of the JadeWeserPort makes exceedingly clear the trouble with classic linear planning, as one finds in nearly all construction, IT, and organizational development projects and companies. A plan, prepared on the basis of forecasts made at a point in time X, sketches out a future. We believe that this is indeed how the future will look. We are aware, however, that things can happen along the way, so we practice systematic risk management and carefully work through change requests. But we almost never consider the fact that the future may be completely different than anything we have even considered.

Once an image of the future has been laid down in our plan, we stubbornly orient ourselves to this single image.

As can be seen quite clearly from the responsible parties' conclusions in the JadeWeserPort example, we tend to stick to our vision of the future even after it has long been obvious that the forecasts haven't held up. We plan on the basis of "established history" – not taking into account the fact that the tomorrow could look very different than yesterday.

In addition to a clear sketch of the future, every good plan provides precise information regarding costs, time-frames, risks, corresponding countermeasures, and quality. We demand credible and crystal-clear statements regarding each of these aspects; we want to know exactly where our project or company will end up. Doubts, alternatives, surprises, and diversity only stand in the way. We want things as simple as possible. Even complicated is okay – however, it is difficult for us to accept that complex processes cannot be described and executed according to a linear plan.

Particularly in the case of project planning, preoccupation with the plan itself can often be seen gaining the upper hand. The participants occupy themselves more with the plan and the planning process than with what really matters. At every meeting, the plan is placed on the table and everyone has a go at it. The plan must be suitable, comprehensive, and always up to date – the plan becomes an end in itself. If, however, any surprises, disturbances, or unexpected twists occur, then it is difficult for many people to deal with them. They shift their focus to what has gone wrong and search for the guilty parties – while continuing to stick to the plan. It is incredibly difficult for responsible parties to admit that their predictions were off the mark or just plain wrong – in other words, that they made an error. Instead, they sidestep the responsibility – "The port was unfortunately launched at the wrong time."

 Another problem with these "conventional" plans is their momentum – they are stubbornly carried through to the end, come what may.

I have listed below the most common factors that take root in the planning stage and end up causing projects to fail.

> **The most common causes of planning disasters:**
>
> ➢ Unexpected obstacles (not captured by risk management)
> ➢ Side effects and interrelationships
> ➢ An isolated approach
> ➢ Incomplete information (in terms of relevance)
> ➢ Pride (of a planner or stakeholder)
> ➢ Focus on hard data
> ➢ Planning based on "old" successes

You may now be asking yourself what one does with a deep-sea port whose originally planned use hasn't worked out. We have already seen some initial steps – theater performances are taking place there, and rotors are being installed for wind turbines in some areas. If the responsible parties think about this, they would have to accept that the whole undertaking made no sense (without being one-hundred-percent sure about it) and that it would have made sense to allow something else to come of it. The price for accepting this would effectively be letting go of the plans that they have followed thus far – and this would be a high price to pay. The next section will be about figuring out how to prevent these "costs" from rising so high in the first place. And this requires looking planning differently when it comes to complex projects.

But first, an important question: How do you deal with planning and with the planning process?

Planning for complexity

How flexible are you when it comes to planning? How do you initiate projects, approach the next sales quarter, or formulate goals for the upcoming fiscal year? Your own attitudes and perspectives are what form the basis for how you decide to proceed. The word "proceed" itself makes us think of procedures, processes, and systematization. Oh, if only there were some tools and techniques that could compensate for our "human weaknesses"!

In the field of software development, some people think that they have found a solution in the form of agile methodology (➡ Glossary). One agile method, for example, is the Scrum (➡ Glossary) framework, which does not actually define a procedural model – but rather roles, activities, and artifacts (documents) that are geared towards making it possible to work in a flexible manner. Agile methods are fundamentally constructed differently than traditional planning. Planning still does happen – but differently. Organizing happens – but differently. Clear roles and responsibilities still exist – but differently. From my perspective, the agile approach is a quite a good one, though it is still nothing more than that. Scrum, for example, is used in many projects as an engineering method; the attitudes and perspectives behind it still conform to the engineering perspective of software production. And thus many agile projects that are launched so ambitiously end up failing, and the approach threatens to combust.

A detailed introduction to agile methodology, or even just to Scrum as its most popular framework, would stretch beyond the scope of this chapter. Below, however, I will highlight just a few essential aspects, presenting them in comparison with the classic approach to projects. The focus here will remain on the topic of planning.

"Always run a changing system," is the motto of the agile community; it reflects the fundamental stance already mentioned above. Software development is seen as a "wicked problem" – a problem with incomplete, contradictory, and changing requirements. It is one in a series of other complex tasks, independent of whether or not it is being worked on in a project organization. In 2001, seventeen renowned software developers signed off on the guiding principles of agile methodology.

The Agile Manifesto

"We are uncovering better ways of developing software by doing it and helping others do it. Through this work we have come to value:

1. *Individuals and interactions* over processes and tools
2. *Working software* over comprehensive documentation
3. *Customer collaboration* over contract negotiation
4. *Responding to change* over following a plan

That is, while there is value in the items on the right, we value the items on the left more."

Planning does not create any value. Thus, agile methodology is in favor of planning only as much as is necessary. What matters more, by comparison, is managing expectations and remaining flexible at all times. At the heart of agile methodology are short iterations – and at the end of each iteration, a working product must be demonstrated. In contrast to the "big bang" approach of classical procedures, work is instead done incrementally in many shorter cycles, and each cycle produces a "usable" result that the customer will either accept or reject.

Each result thus provides input for the next iteration. At the start of each iteration, all participants are committed to the goal. The majority of the time is devoted to implementation – not to refining and perfecting the plan. During the course of an iteration, there are no further demands from the outside; this time is to be stable and undisturbed. An iteration usually lasts only one to eight weeks. Each iteration results in an inspection and a review. A "retrospective" is a meeting in which the team dynamic and the relationship with the customer can (and should) be reflected upon as well.

Planning for the project and for each iteration is handled by the team, not by the project leader or manager. Determining the effort required is done by a different means than usual: starting by establishing the project's scope (size and complexity), which is much easier than stating things immediately in terms of absolute numbers (days, weeks, etc.) Barry W. Boehm laid the foundation for this approach with his function point analysis. If the scope of a task or problem can be estimated, then one can infer from this how much effort will actually be required. It has been shown that this approach leads to faster results. These results are also more realistic, as the experts from the actual team are involved as well. The plan grows more precise over time. It adapts to the reality – instead of vice versa.

> *"One of the most highly developed skills in contemporary Western civilization is dissection: the split-up of problems into their smallest possible components. We are good at it. So good, we often forget to put the pieces back together again."*
> ALVIN TOFFLER

The question that often arises at this point is how to move a project forward without specific cost and time estimates. And therein lies a great misunderstanding with regard to agile approaches. The time-frame and budget are set in advance – what is "flexible" is the performance or functionality. In classical planning, on the other hand, the desired performance or functionality is (more or less well) formulated in advance – while its date of completion then follows from the planning.

In agile projects, the time-frame and budget are fixed, and what will be delivered within this framework is clarified together with the customer. This is precisely why managing expectations is so important. The first plan is always very rough – but what makes it more meaningful right from the start is the fact that it emerges during the course of the project itself, rather than in advance. It emerges from the discussions among the experts and is refined through the first iteration, in which things are already being developed and tested. The first cycles are conducive to experimentation – it's all about finding and rejecting solutions. Safe-fail experiments are carried out.

 Agile planning is rather more "dynamic", if you will, than pure planning.

At the end of the day, it is neither methods nor tools, but rather people's attitudes, that determine whether something will be a success or a failure. All the same, the agile philosophy provides a very good basis for dealing with complex projects and tasks. The agile approach goes far beyond planning and has brought a new realization to the field of software development – namely, that software is developed by people, and that team dynamics thus have a fundamental effect on it. The agile perspective also takes into account the fact that teams are complex and unpredictable. In such a highly structured and mechanical field, these propositions virtually amount to a revolution.

Software development is quite a unique field, and the methods applied there certainly cannot be carried over to other organizational areas – or at least this is what many managers and employees think. In my opinion, this is both true and false in equal measures. Agile philosophy and many of its methodological aspects can be carried over superbly to other complex contexts. As always, though, when it comes to complexity, each individual context must be examined, and the agile processes must be adapted accordingly.

> *"Making plans is often the occupation of an opulent and boastful mind, which thus obtains the reputation of creative genius by demanding what it cannot itself supply, by censuring what it cannot improve, and by proposing what it knows not where to find."*
> IMMANUEL KANT

Scrum and the like are gradually finding their way into other areas of business life; however, they are not yet very well known in the fields of organizational development and strategic management. And yet, principles from software development can be easily extracted for use here. I would like to close this chapter by doing so, adding a few aspects that can assist with planning in complex contexts.

Catalysts for successful planning in complex contexts

➢ Flexibility begins in one's head.
➢ Accept that "There's always something."
➢ Intercommunicate continuously with customers, the market, etc.
➢ Work in short iterations with concrete results.
➢ Allow self-organization to happen; at least self-management as a first step.
➢ Carry out constant reviews / lessons learned.
➢ Create transparency with regard to results, processes, and procedures.
➢ Plan fallback options and redundancies.
➢ Employ future-oriented scenario analysis.

Personally, I don't think much of the occasionally ponderous demands to "get rid of planning completely" and use "only agile". The question of which matters can continue to be planned "classically" and which ones would benefit from a different perspective or process depends on one's particular organizational context. But one thing is irrefutable: Complex matters cannot be planned and executed linearly, because surprises always happen. And regardless of the path you choose: Any model is only as good as the people who are implementing it.

SUMMING UP:

❖ **Planning is taking action in one's mind.**
❖ **The greater the uncertainty, the more meticulous the planning – which leads a person right into the complexity trap.**
❖ **Complex matters cannot be planned linearly.**
❖ **Complexity demands iterative processes, rather than sequential ones.**
❖ **One must have a flexible mindset with regard to methodology and decisions in order to master the handling of complex situations.**

Misconception #6:
The more data you have, the better you will understand

"I demand a swift resolution!" How often have we heard our politicians say such things after some incident? The government just keeps getting hit by one scandal after another, and there's always someone calling for a "swift resolution" to the affair. What does this phrase signify? And what actually happens in response to it?

What it basically means is this: As soon as possible, we are going to find someone at whom we can point our fingers. We are going to start collecting data. A special committee will be brought together and will gather tons of data – so that they can see through this and understand what really happened. And this committee will then figure out who was responsible. For the moment, we are going to focus on this new "understanding" that supposedly emerges from large quantities of data.

By way of example, let's take a look at the scandal surrounding the EuroHawk reconnaissance drone that was ordered for the German Air Force. For those who are unfamiliar: This drone was being developed in cooperation between the companies EADS, which provided the reconnaissance sensors, and Northrop Grumman, which provided the aircraft. The latter company, however, was not able to provide the documentation that would be necessary for certification to operate in European airspace. In mid-May 2013, the German government officially terminated the drone acquisition project, based on the fact that this certification problem would lead to costs ballooning even further.

The details behind this scandal may be highly entertaining, but at the moment we are interested in the question of information-gathering. From June 26 to August 26, 2013, a federal inquiry committee did some reconnaissance of its own, gathering data – a whole lot of data. The committee eventually reached its conclusions on the basis of more than 770 file folders, each one containing up to 400 pages, which were (possibly) reviewed by the approximately 30 members of the committee. Even more data was collected through interviews. This included such details as the fact that "Mr. de Maizière does not use green highlighter pens." This deluge of data led to a finding that the certification problem was already known far in advance.

Does this teach us that gathering lots of data leads to a more complete understanding? No – just that only *relevant* data needs to be reviewed. Because all the way back in 2002, a working group had already submitted its findings report on "Long-range Airborne Surveillance and Reconnaissance," stating that, "The issue of certification for participating in controlled air traffic must be resolved." So, the necessary data was already there, if anyone had bothered to pay attention to it.

It is true that sometimes risks can get overlooked – but I doubt that this was simply a case of overlooking a risk. It's systematic. Something happens (or doesn't happen), and we immediately lapse into a data-gathering frenzy – fueled by hopes of gaining perspective and understanding. We collect as much data as we can – the important thing is having a lot. And whether a particular piece of data is actually relevant doesn't matter.

The EuroHawk affair was far from an isolated case, of course. In the NSU terrorist group scandal, the inquiry committee's August 2013 final report alone contains 1,357 pages. Seriously, who reads (and actually processes) all of that? The inquiry committee in the 2005 German visa affair interviewed 58 witnesses and reviewed 1600 file folders. And for the 9/11 Commission Report, around 2.5 million pages of documents were examined and 1,200 people were interviewed, in order to reach the conclusion that poor agency cooperation helped make the terrorist attacks possible. The upshot? More data gathering. And at the end of the day, everyone interprets the data in their own way.

Quite honestly, this is too much for the human brain. What matters is not the quantity of data, but its relevance – which is something that we can easily overlook, however, when there is just too much to process. We get confused, and we can't see the forest for the trees. Maybe that's just the way we want it – gathering data does make it look like we're busy, after all. It looks like something is getting done. And that's reassuring, isn't it?

The information deficit – A key issue in the information age

Do we really suffer from an information deficit (➡ Glossary)? Is this what drives us to always gather more and more data? The answer to these questions is yes – but at this juncture, we need to distinguish between "data" and "information". The photos on a smartphone, the music on an MP3 player, or the log files on a hard drive are nothing more and nothing less than stored data. They only become information when some sort of meaning is created – when we perceive something in the data.

Data, signals, words, images, bits, and bytes are not necessarily "Information" – one can immediately see this if one looks at cyberneticist Gregory Bateson's definition of the word: "Information is a difference which makes a difference."

 When data generates some sort of meaning or perception in our mind, then we can call it information.

Data decryption happens only in the human mind

Managers have to make decisions in their companies, and the context is non-transparent and highly dynamic. This makes them start to feel like they are missing some information. So they collect more data, hoping that this will help them to make better decisions. However, in a complex environment, they will never manage to gather every single piece of information, nor will they ever be able to gain a complete understanding of a situation. A manager who does not realize this will simply continue to collect more data, because no manager wants to have a potentially wrong decision hanging over his head.

And ultimately, this is what all of the data gathering is about – the fear of making a mistake and having to suffer the consequences. This creates a dilemma that, in the worst-case scenario, can lead to indecision: Gathering more data is intended to provide a clearer understanding, yet this additional data ends up making us aware of even further information deficits, which just results in even more data gathering. It's a vicious cycle.

We still fall victim to the belief that it is possible for us to understand and predict complex systems – if only we collect all of the available data. It is ultimately a reflection of a power struggle as well – those who have the knowledge also have the control and authority. Although such all-encompassing knowledge does not exist anymore when dealing with complex contexts, many managers have not yet fully grasped this.

Confirming one's own knowledge is important

Our data gathering has another motive that also hinders our decision-making. People tend to interpret information in ways that match their past experiences, established beliefs, and convictions – and we sometimes keep looking for new data until we have put together the appropriate information to be able to defend these well to others. This enables us to not only to confirm to ourselves what we already knew, but also to convince those around us. We have long been aware of this psychological phenomenon, known as the "confirmation bias" (➡ Glossary). It has been demonstrated again and again in experiments, including several by leading British cognitive psychologist Peter Cathcart Wason. One of his most famous experiments was the "2-4-6" task.

The experimenter presented participants with the set of numbers 2-4-6. He then asked them to construct their own sets of numbers – and for each set of numbers, they were then told whether or not it conformed to the experimenter's rule. Finally, they were asked to identify the rule. The rule that the experimenter had defined was simply: Three numbers in an ascending sequence.

So, the participants had to form hypotheses and test them. Most started with the sequence 8-10-12, which they were then told conformed to the rule. Afterwards, they would incorrectly assume that the rule was something like "even numbers" or "each number is two greater than the previous number". Most participants used a "positive" strategy, which meant that they kept identifying sets of numbers that they guessed would conform to the rule – which led them to never actually discover the rule itself. On the other hand, following a "negative" strategy – that is, consciously trying to find sets of numbers that did *not* conform to the rule – would have more quickly allowed them to achieve the objective of identifying the actual rule, as it would have opened their thinking much more than repeated confirmations of conforming sets of numbers.

So, our gathering of data and information is also a way for us to substantiate our own subjective truths. We shift our criteria for relevance, paying more attention to data that confirms our preconceived notions, while deeming other data to be "less relevant" – despite the fact that it may be more targeted to our actual ends. In the end, it makes sense that public inquiry committees often reach conclusions that we "knew all along".

 Confirmation bias makes us choose, from among a flood of data, specifically that information which confirms our own opinions.

The volume of data just keeps growing

Each and every one of us is aware that we are constantly using, disseminating, analyzing, and discarding lots of data. But are you also aware of just how much data you actually *create* on a daily basis? Let's take a closer look. Imagine that you are Mr. or Ms. K., an "ordinary" citizen. Your alarm clock wakes you up at 6:30 in the morning, and the first thing you do is turn on your smartphone. Your device connects through the nearest cell tower, recording the exact location where you just woke up. You brush your teeth and then boot up your laptop, so that you can check your emails and read the news while you drink your coffee. All of your time online is logged by your provider, including each and every one of the webpages you visit.

You send a few emails. The recipients and content are stored on your laptop's local hard drive too. An e-mail from a coworker contains a link to a lecture about complexity; you click and watch the video. This data is also logged by your provider. You enjoy the lecture so much that you decide to recommend it to others via Facebook and Google+. Just like all your other online activities, these recommendations are recorded as well.

Then you head to the office. You park near the train station, as you do every day, and send your brother a quick SMS before you board the train. Your cell phone is continuously logged into the network, and your location is known at all times. You arrive at work, start up your computer, and call into a teleconference – more data gets stored. And the fact that you checked your Facebook account and sent two WhatsApp messages during the teleconference is plainly there in the data as well.

On your way home from work, you stop off at the supermarket to buy some ingredients for dinner. You pay with your credit card, and swipe your club card as well. All of the data regarding your purchase gets stored. And you just keep on producing data at home, as you surf the web, use your cell phone, play games online, and stream a movie. We all produce tons of data in this manner, each and every day. So are we accustomed to dealing with such huge quantities of data by now? Well, yes and no. Yes, because we believe that we are living in an information age and that information is king – so the more data, the better! But is that really so? No, because at the same time we still continue to feel like we are suffering from an information deficit.

In 2014, IDC (International Data Corporation), a leading market intelligence firm specialized in the areas of information technology and telecommunications, released a study on "The Digital Universe of Opportunities: Rich Data and the Increasing Value of the Internet of Things". The analysts maintained that, by the year 2020, global data volume would increase to around 44 zettabytes – that's 44 trillion gigabytes. As of 2014, it is around 4.4 trillion gigabytes. This is the sum total of all the photos (selfies, travel photos, snapshots of our lunches) that we upload to Facebook, all the television series we stream, all the data transmitted by probes and sensors (whether from Mars or from the local power plant). It also includes, of course, all of the data that is created and processed within our companies. These are huge and very significant numbers. And the fascinating question behind it all is: How much of this data is actually relevant? And for whom? And for what?

According to IDC, as of 2013, only about 22 percent of all data would be useful if tagged to enable analysis; only 5 percent, however, was actually analyzed. Lots of data – but not much information. By 2020, the analysts projected that the percentage of useful data could rise to 35 percent. The lion's share of this huge stream of data was being created by consumers and employees, i.e., individuals. However, responsibility or liability for 85 percent of the digital universe was held by companies.

As in many IT-focused materials, neither the rapidly escalating quantity of data nor the increasing quality of such data were called into question in the report. The whole thing was formulated as a sort of law of nature by which we, as humans, are bound. The IDC's universal solution is called "big data", which is deemed a must-have for any company that wants to be successful. To quote: "The more data and analytics diversity, the better." (IDC 2014) Better for what? This is unfortunately still an open question, but the figures for the data analytics industry give us a hint – this is already a 40 billion dollar market, and it continues to grow by 10 percent annually. But regardless of who is gaining the most value from this incredible volume of data, the fact is that each of us must deal with constantly increasing amounts of data and information in our organizations.

We are still, for the most part, living in a systematized data-warehouse world. Our data is processed, categorized, and "analyzable". In the future, however, we will increasingly produce volumes of data that are less structured, variously formatted, and of ambiguous value. We will react from a business perspective and seek out the technology necessary to deal with such data. We will invest in relational databases, full-text analysis tools, ontology editors, schema extractor tools, parallel file systems, etc. We will not bother to ask whether we actually need all this data – we will just search for the technical solutions that allow us to manage it.

 We are scared of these huge quantities of data because we know very well that we are unable to process it all.

At the same time, though, we hold such a profound belief that all our answers can be found in the sea of data that we just don't dare to go against the tide. And let's make sure that we distinguish here between the solution and the tools. Big data is not a solution, but rather, at most, just a tool. And it only works as such if we are actually filtering out the relevant data from the constantly increasing flow, interpreting this data, giving it meaning, and thus turning it into real information.

Paradoxically, a "sea of data" leads to an information deficit. Collected data only becomes information when we give it some meaning. However, we cannot give meaning to irrelevant data, which means that it simply remains data without any informational content. This is what gives us the feeling of having an information deficit – which makes us want to gather even more data, instead of simply ignoring the irrelevant data. The problem of extracting relevant data cannot be solved by technical means; rather, it is in the hands of management.

Let me ask you now: What do you do with all the data that you gather and assess in your work nowadays? What do you *really* do with it? We obviously need data and figures in order to successfully manage a department or company and its staff. Business-relevant figures are necessary and proper, of course. But we have gone far beyond this. At an earlier point in my career, as a manager responsible for sales, I wasted lots of time writing different opportunities into my forecasts, complete with percentages and target dates. The half-life period of all this data? One week – i.e., until the next sales meeting.

It makes perfect sense to gather information about your customers. It makes sense to store this information centrally using a CRM system (or a comparable tool), so that the information can always be readily accessed and will remain so even when the employee responsible for it is no longer with the company. It also makes sense to look at this data and to use it for ideas, inferences, proposals, etc. However, it makes no discernible sense to gather information about customers just for the sake of having as large a database as possible, and then to delude yourself into believing that this will enable you to predict how they will think and act.

 No matter how much data you gather, you will not be able to do anything more than identify trends.

In order to do so, however, you must be able to identify the relevant information from your jumble of data. And this is the key point here: Our data gathering is geared towards quantity, but what really matters is relevance (➡ Glossary). And relevance does not automatically emerge from quantity. When we lack clarity or transparency, this cannot be resolved through the quantity of our data – only through its relevance.

Decision-making requires relevant information

As individuals, we are not cut out for processing large quantities of data. Our brain is an organ for problem-solving, not for mass processing. It is, however, remarkably good at identifying relevance – we just need to (want to) use it this way. What would you do if you were to come face-to-face with a lion in the African savanna? You could try the "first gather tons of data" approach, compiling knowledge about lions – average size, weight, hunting behavior, how they rear their young, and so on. You probably wouldn't manage to compile all of this data, though, because the lion would get to you first. Alternatively, you could – and instinctively actually would – activate, in a fraction of a second, the *relevant* information that you have about lions (top of the food chain = acute danger) and run away. Much faster – and, in this case, also more effective.

What we would do in the savanna – harness the relevant information at our disposal – is something that we have forgotten how to do in the course of our everyday managing, where we have come to believe that "more information" means "more perspective and understanding". On the other hand, of course, there are also situations in which we have too little information to manage well and make good decisions.

 The consequences of too much or too little information are the same – a deficiency of actual knowledge.

How can we find relevant information in the sea of data? How can a manager choose properly? These are good questions, especially in light of the fact that we are unable to predict matters and are confronted with a great variety of problems – we may, for example, have to successfully launch a new product, boost our sales for the quarter, find some sort of technical solution, or motivate employees during a transition process.

Let's go back to the Mission Control Center from the film *Apollo 13*. After it became clear that the spacecraft would have to be powered down in order for the rescue of the crew to even stand a chance, the search for a solution began. Such a situation had never occurred before and had not even been envisioned, let alone simulated. The people responsible followed a multi-track strategy: initiating simulations of the new situation, summoning all experts (including those specialized in even the smallest components of the spacecraft), and keeping sight of the big picture. The large-scale analysis phase began.

Another problem quickly emerged – the crew had to change over to the lunar module, which was not designed to supply the whole crew with oxygen for several days. The only solution seemed an impossible task: connecting the command module's square CO_2 filter to the round receptacle of the lunar module's ventilation system. A group of experts worked on solving this problem using only the materials and objects inside the spacecraft. Over the course of this work, their discussions were sharply focused on the information that was relevant to their goal.

You may now argue that the problem in this case was very clear and that it was thus easy to identify what information was relevant – but what about, for example, the launch of a new product? It can only work with the appropriate analyses of the market, customers, target groups, trends, etc. The answer is that even such analyses will only allow one to predict the complex system of "the market" on a limited basis.

It is impossible to guarantee, a priori, the success of any product or action.

It is easy to see retroactively the cause-and-effect relationships that have produced such success. So other information is needed in order to avoid simply trying things randomly, but rather to carry out well-founded experiments in the market – for example, by replicating proven patterns and models. If you have identified a link between successful ringtones and animal sounds, then you can offer a seal-barking ringtone.

But this makes you a copycat, and is not enough if you want to be a pioneering innovator in the market. Instead of just analyzing reports, you need to have a sense of what is going on in your field – you must have a certain empathy for the market. Apple, with its longtime visionary Steve Jobs, is a prime example of market empathy. The iPod success story began in October 2001, when Jobs surprised everyone by introducing a new MP3 player that was capable of storing 1,000 songs. Its design was completely different from the competitors in the market – it was small, had only a few buttons, contained a hard drive, and fit in one's pants pocket. The iPod paved the way for the success of all of the later iProducts.

Let's take a step back now to shine a light on the context. When Steve Jobs returned to Apple in 1997, the company was floundering. The iMac was introduced one year later, in May 1998, and more than 300,000 were sold in its first 45 days. It was different from all of the other boring, grey computers on the market – it was colorful and cool, and it was the first computer that really spoke to the youth. Its success was partly due to Steve Jobs' intuition regarding this particular demand.

> *"The intuitive mind is a sacred gift and the rational mind is a faithful servant. We have created a society that honors the servant and has forgotten the gift."*
> ATTRIBUTED TO ALBERT EINSTEIN

In 1999, Napster popularized the online exchange of music; people around the world used the service to download songs in the MP3 format. Soon afterwards, the first portable MP3 players reached the market, allowing people to take their music with them anywhere. Incidentally, Sony, which had been a pioneer in portable music technology with its Walkman, completely missed out on this opportunity – Apple, however, did not. The company introduced iTunes in January 2001 to meet the demand for MP3 music, especially amongst the younger generation. Just nine months later, the iPod was launched.

The timing was extremely unfavorable. Napster lost a lawsuit that had been brought against it by the music industry, the dot-com bubble had long burst, and the September 11 attacks dampened people's spirit of consumption. But what mattered was that Apple had generated a resonance in the market, with a combination of cool design and MP3 music. The iMac's design concept (clear, simple, and easy to use), when combined with the iTunes music service, created momentum and triggered enthusiasm that went far beyond Mac users.

> *"You can't just ask customers what they want and then try to give that to them. By the time you get it built, they'll want something new."*
> STEVE JOBS

If you will be involved in implementing any important changes at your company in the near future, you may be occupying yourself with change management issues – and you will have undoubtedly experienced and learned about the great importance of information in change processes. However, in my personal experience, even when dealing with change management, it is often more about data than actual information. Many managers ask themselves: What information should we pass on to whom, when, and in what form? It can't be too much, because employees could get overwhelmed, and it can't be too little, because everyone needs to be aware of what's going on.

Unfortunately, those responsible for such processes often see matters through "management glasses". They dispense politically filtered bits of information, which then gets presented in the form of brochures or roadshows. The resonance is low, and only a small percentage of people are truly reached. Very few of them get enthused and motivated in this manner. But wherein lies the crux? When choosing information to disseminate, do we simply choose incorrectly? Or too little?

How resonance can be generated within the system of our company is something that we usually cannot know in advance – and as long as we don't know this, the dissemination of information often simply happens by "trial and error". It might go well, but not necessarily. How points of resonance can be discovered has been demonstrated by the Otto Group, with its global project geared towards strengthening its group of companies.

Tens of thousands of motivated people

In 2004, the Otto Group's HR, marketing, and business communications departments determined that the group urgently needed to bolster the sense of unity among its employees. At the time, the company employed around 55,000 people in 19 countries, organized into more than 100 companies.

Strengthening the spirit of unity within a company requires working with values, because shared goals and values are what bring people together. In one common approach to such a project, the management will draft a list of "core values", following this up with whatever measures they deem appropriate to communicate these guiding values to everyone at the company. Lots of data is produced and distributed in the process, but it often does not have much effect.

Instead, it is better to involve people in order to find out what actually appeals to them – and so, the Otto Group chose a different path. Middle managers were interviewed in order to ascertain the values that prevailed among the group's individual companies. An analytical process was used to generate a common value map from the interview results. The values specifically identified in this manner were passion, innovation, integrated networking, and sustainability. Project leaders were now aware of the most significant points of resonance within the organization – and knew that they had to take actions that addressed these areas if they wanted to inspire stronger identification on the part of employees.

And the company chose an unusual – and ultimately highly successful – way of accomplishing this. Under the title "Otto Group Milestones – Achieving More Together", employees were asked to paint stones and send them to the company's headquarters in Hamburg. Each of the group's individual companies implemented the campaign on its own, with the managers of each company given responsibility for motivating their own employees. Their initiatives included setting out paint buckets, special themed meals in the company cafeteria, and even a "stone party". For each stone received, the Otto Group donated three Euros to a children's charity. Those who had painted the three best stones, as selected by a special jury, were awarded 5,000 Euros each.

By the end of the initiative, more than 33,600 stones lined the lobby of the Otto Group's headquarters in Hamburg. The project incorporated the four values that had been identified earlier: sustainability (using stones), networking (cooperation, the "stone party"), innovation (the initiative itself), and passion (some genuine works of art were produced). The company had involved its employees and spoken to the values that they already shared, implementing a collective campaign in order to bring them closer together.

 When we know what motivates people, then we can trigger these points in order to create resonance. Without prior knowledge of what points to trigger, however, our efforts might remain nothing more than streams of data.

Finding and extracting relevant information is one thing. But how can we determine what will eventually become relevant? In a flood of information, how can we filter out precisely *the* snippets of information that may develop into something relevant in the future?

Weak signals – The harbingers of opportunities and risks

No matter what recent scandal or crisis you look at, there were prior warning signs. From EuroHawk to 9/11, weak signals were already appearing long in advance every time. So when it came to the EuroHawk project, for example, how could the intelligent people working for the German Ministry of Defense and the involved companies have allowed the whole affair to end up happening? Did they not see the signals? Did they not want to see them?

In November 1999, representatives of the German Ministry of Defense and armed forces visited Edwards Air Force Base in California to observe a test flight of the Global Hawk (as the drone was then known); the test flight was cancelled two days before the scheduled date due to software problems. And this was not the first time that such problems had arisen. In March 1999, a Global Hawk drone had been destroyed when it crashed after receiving incorrect signals. Nevertheless, in March 2000, the go-ahead was given to start official discussions and assess the Global Hawk. In a December 1999 paper to Germany's then-Secretary of State, reference was already made to potential certification problems: "The formulation of the certification criteria for flying in common airspace has proven to be problematic for the deployment of high-flying unmanned drones."

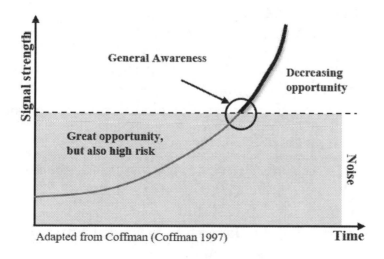

Weak signals are harbingers.

A key reason for the failure of the project was the lack of an anti-collision system, which is strictly required for flights in European airspace. Experts had pointed this out repeatedly since at least 2004. Without an anti-collision system, only flights in closed airspace are permitted – such as the test flight that took place in German territory in 2005. There were major technical difficulties during this flight too, with the drone occasionally wobbling uncontrollably in the air. Experts from the German armed forces travelled to California again in 2009; production of the drone had already been completed by this time, so it was no longer possible to review its functionality. It took until mid-2013 before the project was declared a (partial) failure and was terminated; 600 million Euros had been invested in the project by then.

In such cases, the news coverage tends to only identify the guilty parties and attest to their incompetence or human error. This, however, is very short-sighted. Taking another look at these processes, with a focus on perceptions, preconceptions, and groupthink, can help us better deal with early warmings and weak signals. Perceptions, assessments, interpretations, conclusions, and decisions happen on both the individual and organizational levels – and both are worth observing.

Objectivity is an illusion

We like to claim that we are able to observe and judge situations objectively. Pure objectivity (➡ Glossary), however, is an illusion.

 Managers need to be aware of thinking traps when making their assessments and conclusions, because each and every one falls victim to such pitfalls.

Confirmation bias is one such common trap that was discussed earlier. We choose information that matches our preconceived notions, and we interpret it accordingly – while subconsciously blocking out information that does not match our expectations.

Another such trap is selective perception, a psychological phenomenon that manifests itself when we are focused intensely or are in a non-transparent environment. Psychologist Daniel J. Simons developed the popular "gorilla experiment", which is now standard in management trainings. In this test, a video is shown in which players in white and black shirts pass basketballs around. The person watching the video is asked to simply count how many passes are made by the players wearing white shirts. In the middle of the video, a gorilla walks into the middle of the action, thumps its chest, and then leaves.

Around 50 percent of those who watch the video do not notice the gorilla. They are busy counting passes, and they block out any "unnecessary" information. In another version of the gorilla video, curtains in the background change color and a member of the black-shirted team leaves the scene – and even people who are familiar with the first video, and thus now notice the gorilla, still fail to notice the other changes that occur during the course of the video. They do not seem relevant to the actual objective (counting passes by white-shirted players), so they are blocked out or simply missed.

The more we focus our attention, the more severe our tunnel vision becomes. We should be conscious of this fact – and we should train our minds to allow more details and information in. Paying attention to weak signals means being aware – being aware of the mechanisms by which we observe, interpret, and assess things, and being aware of our environment and what is happening within it.

 Note that even when we are aware of the emotional and cognitive filters through which all information reaches us, we still are not at all objective.

We draw conclusions from data and we make value judgments about situations, statements, people, and groups. Biases emerge – through rationalization, for example, as we find conclusive arguments to retroactively explain events or situations, interpreting the facts in such a manner that they fit our prior beliefs. This is also what happens when we try to find reasons why someone else has made an error, or when we observe any other such external circumstances.

We sometimes get caught in the "wishful thinking" trap, seeing the world in a too-positive light and suppressing potentially negative facts. In other cases, we fall victim to the so-called "fundamental attribution error", placing relatively more importance on people's internal characteristics than on external factors. And we also may succumb to the egocentrism trap, viewing others' behavior only in relation to our own – sometimes even going so far as to believe that we are the center of the action, interpreting all events exclusively from our own perspective.

With a constant influx of information that occasionally confuses us, we sometimes seek out those who will confirm our opinions – and even reinforce them. You may have noticed people going to great efforts to find others who are like-minded – for example, starting everything they say in meetings with phrases like

"Don't you agree that...", as a way of seeking reinforcement. And if the person doing so is the boss, then his employees will typically answer "yes", even if they actually have some reservations on the matter.

Such an approach can basically lead to a person's views becoming so firm that he stops seeking or even considering any other information. Even in retrospect, such a person will represent the situation in the way that most suits him. Hindsight bias is one of the most common biases, making us adjust our original opinions and assessments to the eventual factual outcome. After the fact, we say that "we knew it all along!", overestimating the predictability of the event and the causes behind it.

Why group decisions are not always better

The Bay of Pigs invasion began on April 17, 1961, with 1,300 Cuban exiles landing on the island nation's shores in a CIA-sponsored campaign. The goal of the campaign was to overthrow Fidel Castro. However, perceptions of Castro's army turned out to be not only vague, but wrong – it was thought that a surprise attack would bring the Cuban armed forces to collapse, but no one was aware of the actual strength of the country's troops. Among the most crucial false assumptions made by the group that surrounded President John F. Kennedy was the notion that the Cuban air force was weak and could be eliminated quickly. The U.S.A. was aware that Castro had Soviet bomber jets at his disposal, but assumed that these were not yet ready for service. The experienced Czech pilots who had been in Cuba since October 1960 were forgotten as well.

Shortly before the start of the invasion, Kennedy withdrew U.S. military backing of the Cuban exiles and reaffirmed his public statement that there would never be any military intervention on the part of the United States. Based on information from unsupported sources, the U.S.A. presumed that about 2,400 underground fighters were prepared to fight. The whole series of miscalculations eventually led to the disaster in the Bay of Pigs. Faulty planning and poor communication were probably the group of experts' biggest mistakes.

How could such highly qualified people have failed to verify information and make well-founded decisions?

The basic assumption of the groupthink (➡ Glossary) phenomenon is the development of an extremely strong sense of unity within the group. As a result, shared illusions sometimes end up seeming so truthful that the group no longer bothers to question or verify them.

The group begins to consider itself invulnerable and take increasingly greater risks.

"It seemed that, with John Kennedy leading us and with all the talent he had assembled, nothing could stop us. We believed that if we faced up to the nation's problems and applied bold, new ideas with common sense and hard work, we would overcome whatever challenged us." These are the words of a Justice Department confidant, based on discussion of the initiative with Robert Kennedy on the day it was launched. The euphoria that emerges among a group makes rational decision-making almost impossible. Shared perspectives are considered truth and, worse yet, reality. If any individual does have critical thoughts, he does not express them – no one wants to be seen as weak or antagonistic. For the individual group members, the harmony within the group eventually becomes more important than their own opinions or any possible risks. The groupthink effect undermines the otherwise inherently positive effects of collective knowledge.

Janis (1982) identified seven mistakes made by groups in decision-making situations:

1. Incomplete survey of alternatives
2. Incomplete survey of objectives
3. Failure to examine risks of preferred choice
4. Failure to reappraise initially rejected alternatives
5. Poor information search
6. Selective bias in processing information at hand
7. Failure to work out contingency plans

However strong or weak any signals may be, they only make sense when they are made a subject of the discussion and when the pieces of the puzzle are then put together. This requires cooperation, diversity, and the free flow of information.

In the five months leading up to the September 11 terrorist attacks, the Federal Aviation Administration (FAA) received a total of 105 reports from the CIA, the FBI, and the U.S. State Department, in which "Osama Bin Laden" or "Al Qaeda" appeared around 52 times. These reports were sent to various U.S. authorities – unfortunately, this does not automatically mean that they were brought together and meaningful conclusions drawn from them. Some of these notices were relayed to local authorities, others were not. The end result was that the terror risk was not recognized in advance (at least not to its full extent), despite the presence of signals.

Managing boldly in a sea of data

The hoarding of knowledge as power, as often happens in our complex, dynamic, workplaces, is neither reasonable nor effective. No individual, not even a great manager, can fully grasp a complex system. Yet we are constantly confronted with a barrage of data and the constant noise that accompanies it – and we are forced to make decisions with "limited visibility". In order to succeed in doing so, there are a few aspects to which attention should be paid:

What to watch out for when dealing with tons of data:

➢ Holding back information harms the system, resulting in an information deficit among employees and colleagues.
➢ An excess of data also harms the system, resulting in an information deficit among employees and colleagues.
➢ Relevant information is needed for decision-making.
➢ Train your feel for the market, for your employees, and for trends.
➢ Involve your employees, instead of just overwhelming them with data.
➢ Keep up a dialogue with your employees in order to learn what motivates them.
➢ Be alert to confirmation bias, selective perception, wishful thinking, and groupthink.

Before we start collecting even more data, we need to come to grips with the mechanisms by which we select, interpret, and manipulate data – and we need to learn to recognize relevance.

SUMMING UP:

❖ **We are constantly being subjected to a flood of data – but a deficit of information.**
❖ **We can only analyze a limited amount of data; floods of information are not helpful.**
❖ **Our brains are masters at filtering out relevant information.**
❖ **Weak signals are harbingers of opportunities and risks.**
❖ **Changes and crises always foreshadow themselves.**

Misconception #7:
Trust is good,
control is better

He sits at the head of the table, as befits a man of his position. All around him, his closest confidants have taken their places. His gaze wanders from one to the next, his hands resting on the table, his eyes piercing yet calm. All who are met by his glare look down at the floor instinctively. He is the man responsible for the many who are under his leadership. He has ambitious goals, and he is willing to take risks.

Those who report directly to him are loyal and strong-willed – sort of like chained watchdogs. They are always alert – ready for anything. He often stands over his men and watches them toil away. Many of the assignments he gives them are largely intended to advance the principles he most values – obedience, discipline, and subordination. The slightest deviations from his rules, even if unintentional, are immediately and ruthlessly castigated. No one should even think of not following his orders. He can never allow himself to lose control.

Fast forward: His plans are up against some serious turbulence. Everything is in disarray and his men are anxious and panicking. One of his top officers suggests that he change course, steer back towards calmer waters. But he refuses – he is determined to stay the course. He brushes aside all the warnings. And when asked how long the men are expected to endure, he replies that they must endure as long as their superiors do. No matter the cost, his ambition prevents him from changing course and losing time.

And so it goes. Through easy times and rough times alike, he remains true to his approach. Some of his top men start getting their own ideas, but he doesn't like this – he insists on unconditional obedience of his rules and decorum. Even when he feels like he is being driven into a corner, his only strategy is "more of the same". And eventually it all comes to a head, as the inevitable happens – a mutiny on the *Bounty*. Captain Bligh is forced off the ship, together with his most loyal watchdogs.

Oh wait – that whole story was just from a Hollywood retelling of an 18th-century historical incident? What does any of this have to do with the realities of the modern-day business world? Well, perhaps more than we would like. Some companies nowadays have their own Captain Blighs – although most are somewhat better disguised and more strategic in their actions. But just like on the *Bounty*, these commanders all too often try to maintain control over everything in a department or a company. They want to know everything, see everything, decide everything, and run a tight ship.

But certainly not as tyrannically as the tragic character from the film, right? Ah, if only. On the *Bounty*, the seamen got special ration dinners after successfully passing through storms. In our own organizations, we call such things "incentives" or "perks". They are the "carrots" – and although I admittedly have never seen employees literally get the "stick" (or be tied to a mast), I certainly do see the modern variants of such punishments. Publicly lambasting team members, marginalizing them, or setting them up for failure by withholding information – these are all common sorts of "sticks".

Captain Bligh's leadership style would probably be described as authoritarian. But where would such a leadership style even be learned nowadays? To my knowledge, there are no seminars that preach authoritarian management. I've never seen any promotional materials advertising: "Learn how to be tyrannical in our three-day training course: Everything you need to know in order to subdue your employees and keep absolute control!" If you ask anyone in any company what leadership style they favor, everyone will say things like "cooperative" or "participative". No manager will readily admit to running his ship like Captain Bligh and thinking that this is a good thing. But the more you look, the more you see micromanagement, constant surveillance, mistrust, punishment, etc. So again: If no one wants it, teaches it, or admits to using it, then why do we constantly see this management style manifest itself in our organizations? Funny, isn't it?

Seeking heroes

In the story of the mutiny on the *Bounty*, the tyrannical Captain Bligh plays the role of the villain. Opposing him is Fletcher Christian, who is good, charismatic, and has a strong sense of justice – the hero of the story. Essentially responsible for the mutiny, he eventually wants to return and testify before a military court. And the crew, loyal and motivated, certainly would have followed him. Every good story needs a hero. This has always been the case, and always will be. It's what we all yearn to be.

"When I grow up..."

Ever since we were children, there have been heroes all around us – in fairy tales, comic books, films, and fables. Who were your childhood heroes? Peter Pan, Superman, Robin Hood, maybe even Lassie? Whoever they were, they gave you a sense of direction and security. Our heroes teach us which values make a person good. They give us ideas about who and what we want to be. This is GOOD, that is BAD – it's simple. Heroes go on lots of adventures, excel at what they do, make the impossible possible, always solve every problem, and usually rescue others. They nurture our longing for success, as this is one thing that they all have in common – they are all successful at what they do.

Even now, as adults, our search for heroes continues. We find them in the business world, in politics, or in the entertainment industry. Most recently in 2009, the Harris Interactive Corporation has surveyed Americans to find out who they admire enough to consider a hero (Harris, 2009). As of that year, Barack Obama took the number one spot, followed by Jesus and then Martin Luther King. God fell out of the top ten, coming in at number 11. Oprah Winfrey and Bill Gates took 20th and 23rd place respectively. Survey respondents were also asked what aspects of these people made them heroes – and the following were the top five characteristics named:

> *Doing what's right regardless of personal consequences (89%)*
> *Not giving up until the goal is accomplished (83%)*
> *Doing more than what other people expect of them (82%)*
> *Overcoming adversity (82%)*
> *Staying level-headed in a crisis (81%)*

Some other "heroic" characteristics may come to your own mind – and while you may not consider the people named above to be your own heroes, there are certainly others who are heroes from your perspective. In the public eye, there are many different kinds of people who are frequently deemed heroes and (albeit less frequently) heroines. Edward Snowden – a hero of the digital age. Steve Jobs – a hero and philanthropist. Yulia Tymoshenko – a heroine of the West. These are some of our current heroes. And like the idols of our childhood, they give us a sense of direction and gratify our desire for success.

From comic books to the daily newspapers, there are many similarities between the various "heroic" images that are presented to us. The hero is often seen as a "lone wolf", an outsider, tough but fair. He is feared, admired, celebrated, and loved. He fights for what is good, and he (almost) always wins. And one essential aspect of all our heroes: They seem to have everything under control. The hero takes control of the situation, of the crisis, the chaos. And now, we are at the crux of the matter – and we have the reason why complexity does *not* require heroes.

Heroes want to make sure that they have everything under control – every single detail, if possible. Many managers are the same.

Everything under control!?

We all sometimes fall victim to notions that we can control things over which we objectively have no power – and this is true regardless of whether the situation is complex or not. It is an illusion that can motivate us, just like many positive illusions. In the 1980s, Harvard University psychology professor Ellen Langer was the first to study this phenomenon. For example, she observed that people who played the lottery gave themselves better chances of winning when they had carefully chosen the numbers themselves. The phenomenon was also evident at the craps table, with people throwing dice more forcefully when they wanted higher numbers, but more softly when they wanted lower numbers. And the more a person can intervene and take decisions, the greater his illusion of being able to control matters. But what gives us this penchant for control? What purpose does it serve?

Psychologist Icek Ajzen's "Theory of Planned Behavior" gives us an answer to this question. According to this theory, a perception of control (i.e., an *internal* locus of control ➡ Glossary) is necessary for a person to even act at all. A person who does not feel like it is possible for him to control things (i.e., *external* locus of control) usually does not move past the intention to act. This subjectively perceived control can be completely different from the objective reality. The more familiar we are with a topic, problem, or organization, the more we believe that it is possible for us to control the respective matters personally.

The illusion of control motivates us to act. It gives us certainty. Without it, we would remain inactive in many situations. This is closely related to our self-efficacy (➡ Glossary): To what extent do we believe that we can achieve something through our actions and thus influence our environment? How much of a role do we think that we ourselves play in how effective we are? The crucial factor is not how much influence our behavior objectively has – but rather how much we believe in our own efficacy.

The urban noise experiment (Glass 1972) makes this quite clear. Three separate groups of test subjects were each given the same proofreading task, with all participants being exposed to loud street noise during the entire time. The first group was given the option of shutting off the noise by pressing a button. The second group was given the same option, although they were asked to avoid using the button if at all possible. The third group had no such button. The experiment sought to discover which group would produce the best results, and why.

The third group performed the worst; the participants in this group felt like they had no control over the situation. The first two groups performed better, at similar levels; all participants in these groups had the option of taking action to shut off the noise. What the test subjects in the second group did not know, however, was that their button did not actually do anything – i.e., it was enough for them to simply believe that they could influence the situation.

Self-efficacy refers to an individual's belief that they can accomplish a particular activity. This influences one's own perceptions, motivations, and actual performance. It is often equated with locus of control – however, this is inaccurate. Locus of control relates to the belief that one's behavior is somehow capable of controlling events; self-efficacy relates to the belief in actually being able to bring about a specific event. Both of these convictions have a significant influence on our behavior.

Control, self-efficacy, and action

➤ Person A believes that it is impossible to increase sales figures in the upcoming quarter, because no suitable ideas for doing so exist (external locus of control, no self-efficacy) ➡ will not act.
➤ Person B believes that the sales figures can be increased, but she herself has no ideas for doing so (internal locus of control, but no self-efficacy) ➡ will not act, but may involve someone else.
➤ Person C believes that the sales figures can be increased, and she has suitable ideas for doing so (internal locus of control, self-efficacy) ➡ will act immediately.
➤ Person D believes that it is impossible to increase the sales figures, despite the fact that she has suitable ideas (external locus of control, thus no self-efficacy) ➡ will not act.

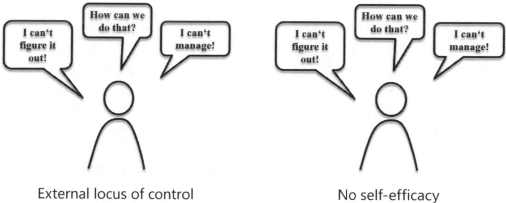

External locus of control | No self-efficacy

Control and self-efficacy can be illusory convictions that have nothing to do with reality, but they are important motivators for us. We may succumb to the illusion of control when faced with simple or complicated tasks, as well as complex tasks – but the situation is hopeless in this latter case, because:

 In complex systems, control is always an illusion.

The days of the old-fashioned heroes are gone

The lone wolf has had his day. The hero who spends his life fighting for his values and goals, who always manages to see through everything and take all the right decisions on his own – it may still work for him on the big screen, but his role has become obsolete in our modern-day business world. Complexity requires leaders and managers who integrate, rather than command – who facilitate, rather than control.

Are you familiar with Gene Kranz? Many of you have heard of him through the film *Apollo 13*, in which he was portrayed by Ed Harris. Kranz was a NASA Flight Director during the Apollo program. Both in real life and in the film, Kranz is a "modern hero" as the savior of the Apollo 13 crew – he was largely responsible for their successful return to Earth. In the process, however, he acted much more inconspicuously than we usually expect from heroes. After an oxygen tank aboard the spacecraft exploded, the problem was solved on the ground under Kranz's leadership. Or rather, the problems were solved – as the explosion actually resulted in several major problems. Kranz understood the extent of the calamity and, even more importantly, accepted it as such. He gathered the core members of the team and told them to forget all the plans – from then on, they would be improvising a new mission.

"Failure is not an option."
GENE KRANZ IN APOLLO 13

It was clear that the lunar landing mission would have to be aborted prematurely – the first question now was how to get the spacecraft back to Earth. Make a direct U-turn or loop around the moon? Kranz let the experts debate everything, listened to the options, and then decided which of these options should be examined in more detail, which analyses should be carried out, and which experts should be brought in. He was ready to alter his decisions at any time, in the event that conditions were to change, and to permit new ideas and solutions, as crazy as they might sound to him. His most important decision-making tools were experience, intuition, and trust. This is how he dealt with all of the serious problems that arose, from the power supply to the loss of oxygen to the question of how to connect the command module's square filters to the lunar module's round receptacles.

 The type of hero that we need now has changed – from the lone wolf to the "integrative facilitator".

But Apollo 13 was a matter of life or death, you may now be thinking. Sure it was, but that makes no difference – there is a lot that we can learn from this example, even if lives are not at stake in our own day-to-day work. There is always something at stake – success in a complex world, adaptability to constantly changing conditions, or the survival of a company, for example. Now, the question is: What does this mean for management and leadership in complex contexts?

Management means regulating, not controlling

Production of the Ford Model T began in 1908 – and by the following year, it would revolutionize both the automobile market and industrial production processes. Henry Ford had a vision of making the automobile accessible to all, and he intended to make this vision a reality with the Model T. Up to then, car production had been laborious and expensive – speeding up the process was to help make them affordable for all Americans.

Henry Ford understood that he would have to cut production costs by changing processes in order to achieve his goal. He organized production lines, following the model of slaughterhouses; this sped up the process, but it still was not enough. Then, he hired Frederick Taylor (➡ Glossary), who was working intensively at the time on the question of how to improve efficiency in industrial processes. After studying the processes and procedures in place at Ford's company, Taylor recommended that tasks be assigned on the basis of each worker's own capabilities and strengths, and that all unnecessary physical movement by the workers be eliminated.

Ford adapted Taylor's recommendations and fundamental management theories, as he began reconstructing his assembly process, step by step. Large parts were now to remain stationary, while smaller parts would be brought to the car; this change further sped up the production, but it still was not enough for Ford. He then had the cars pulled through the assembly line using a rope, so that assembly workers would not have to move around anymore. And after these and many other such changes, each of which contributed towards optimizing the process, a completely power-driven assembly line for the Model T was introduced in 1913 – and an automobile that earlier required 12 hours of production time could now be completed in 93 minutes.

The purchase price for the Model T dropped, and the car became affordable for many more Americans. Ford raked in substantial profits. In 1917, the company began construction of the River Rouge Plant, which became the largest industrial facility in the world upon its completion. There, 10,000 Model Ts rolled off the assembly line each day, assembled by 100,000 workers. Obviously, however, not everything was perfectly rosy in this success story. For a long time, the company did not need to hire any more skilled employees, as production had been broken up into the smallest possible steps, each of which could be performed by any unskilled worker – so the management determined the speed of assembly line and thus the pace of each employee's work, without any room for discussion or negotiation. Even going to the toilet required the permission of one's supervisor. Many workers stayed on the job for only a few weeks, before the monotony and high workload drove them elsewhere.

Henry Ford's response to this was raising salaries – he paid five dollars per day, basically double what other companies were paying at the time. He certainly did not do this merely because he was a good person and wanted to retain his workers – he wanted each of them to be able to afford a Model T as well. He vehemently refused to accept unions in his company, and dismissed any employees who wanted to join one. He believed in good money as a reward for hard work. Everything took a backseat to the Ford system, and the rules of the system had to be followed.

Henry Ford's story serves as an illustration of many things: the American dream, the self-made man, the visionary, the revolutionary – and also of controlling management. Ford wanted to manipulate his company in such a way that he could control the behavior of everyone involved. There were no feedback mechanisms – in fact, these were strictly avoided. Control was an important tool for Ford. He controlled the work schedules, automobile parts, processes, people, unions, breaks, even trips to the toilet. There was no room for the workers' ideas, which were unnecessary in Ford's opinion. The analyses that were carried out were sufficient to design the most efficient possible process for maximizing profitability.

The first Model T was produced more than a century ago – and control, discipline, efficiency, reliability, and accuracy are still considered essential values in the management of our companies today.

 The idea of being able to control a company in the style of Henry Ford is still firmly anchored in many people's minds.

This is mostly due to the fact that improving efficiency is still very important to us. We say that we have to increase productivity or double our sales – as if there were no outside forces that affected this. But we are not working in the automobile market of the early 1900s – we are facing the complex, dynamic challenges of the 21st century. We are not dealing with the linear production of identical products, but rather with extensive interrelationships between things that we cannot decide or control ourselves. We eventually have to accept this – as well as the fact that the methods used back then are thus no longer compatible with the tasks of today.

The challenges of regulating complex systems

I will now once again cite the basic features of complex systems, which were explained in detail in the introductory chapter, in order to outline here the hurdles that they present for management. Complexity is the great challenge of our times – and this results in a variety of difficulties and problems when it comes to managing organizations.

Non-linearity results in unpredictability

Henry Ford was able to take apart the Model T's production process in order to understand and optimize the individual steps involved. Assembling such a car was complicated – and thus linear. In complex systems, however, things cannot just be taken apart. Each and every manager must face this fact and ask himself, "Am I able and willing to deal with this?"

Managers who have climbed the corporate ladder mostly on the merits of their expertise tend to be more comfortable in the orderly, linear world, and should thus consider pursuing a specialist career track. Unpredictability always involves uncertainty about how things will be tomorrow, and this has a significant impact on how decisions are to be made and how employees are to be led.

Interconnectedness and system dynamic

Everything is interconnected with everything else. Most people will just nod and agree with this – but what does this actually mean for how we manage? Does it mean that we basically don't need to do anything? No, quite the contrary. The desire for control is often a hindrance to networking, as managers who want to control everything tend to actively prevent networking from taking place, thus disturbing the system (in a negative way). They impede employees from communicating with department X, keeping colleague Y in the loop, or getting input from team Z – this is what actively interfering with a system's interconnectedness looks like. However, the indiscriminate interconnection of everything and everyone can be just as detrimental. It is not about aimlessly interconnecting together as much as possible – but rather about ensuring that the system is networked in the most goal-oriented manner, remaining conscious of its unpredictable nature.

Additionally, complex systems develop a certain dynamic on their own. They do not wait for decisions or stimuli from management. They are constantly evolving, with their interconnectedness generating effects and repercussions. This means that management is on the spot – they must make decisions as soon as possible, because if decisions are not made or are made too late, then the project will be left to its own dynamic with nothing actively regulating it.

Interconnectedness and system dynamic result in non-transparency

Let's quickly recall NASA Flight Director Gene Kranz. Even just the interrelationships among the technical equipment in the command and lunar modules were too much for him to fully grasp and comprehend alone – it was too complex. So Kranz had to reach decisions despite lacking lots of information at hand. Non-transparency is a feature of complex systems that renders decision-making particularly challenging. The fact that the system is dynamic means that we must consider not only its current state, but rather also how it will evolve in the future. This means operating with many unknowns.

Self-organization is not made – it develops

We often stand in the way of self-organization. Many people in managerial positions think that self-organization is something that they need to actively initiate or allow. But that is not how it works – every complex system, particularly social systems such as teams or departments, functions in a self-organized manner. This does not mean that managers can just sit back and relax with a laissez-faire attitude – on the contrary, self-organization is grounded in clear rules and processes.

A company, a department, a project, or any other such system has a job to fulfill. In order to accomplish this, it must be constantly assessed by management and its patterns must be corrected as necessary via continuous feedback into the system. Self-organization only "works" if all participants in the system (are able to) assume their responsibilities, clear-cut interactions take place, and a high degree of transparency is established.

Feedback is the regulating mechanism

The main difference between controlling and regulating lies in providing feedback into the system. Feedback is a tool that is always at our disposal, although unfortunately many managers have not yet fully recognized its significance – it is the only regulating mechanism that we have in complex systems. The upshot of every action or decision also functions as input for the next action or decision. Why do we often not want to see or hear this?

To put it simply, incorporating feedback in complex environments often means reviewing decisions and changing course. Positive feedback tells us, "Everything is being done properly – carry on." This is what we want to hear; we can continue to follow the same path. Negative feedback tells us, "Something is unsatisfactory – changes are necessary." This is not what we want to hear, as it makes us uncomfortable. No feedback at all tells us nothing more than, "Okay, carry on" – there is an implicit positive feedback here that reinforces without actually regulating. For example, seeing enough individual instances of people come late to meetings, if it is never addressed, will eventually lead to an unspoken rule that "it's okay to come late to meetings – you can do as you please."

 Negative feedback is regulation in the strictest sense, and is thus a fundamental task of management.

Making decisions without certainty

Managers have to make decisions. That is their job – and it is precisely here that the complexity of their projects and organizations catches up to them, because the certainty that exists when making decisions in complicated contexts no longer exists in complex contexts. The question that then arises is – how do I make my decisions in complex environments? Knowledge and predictability cannot form the basis of decision-making here; rather, the decision-making mechanism in complex systems is as follows: Perform tests – observe results – respond accordingly.

I have already discussed testing in the chapter on misconception #4. Now, however, another question comes to the fore: How do I choose the right experiments and tests? The answer – collective intuition. The individual experience of individual managers cannot form the basis for such decisions, because our experience always comes from distinct contexts. If the situation at hand presents a different context, then directly transferring one's prior experiences makes little sense – and could lead to bad decisions. We need the intuition of the system, of its various participants. Moving from solitary decision-making to utilizing collective intuition meets the requirements of Ashby's Law – complex answers for complex problems.

Leading without certainty

Employees need a sense of direction, and they get this from their managers. This is true – but it does not mean that employees always need 100% certainty and predictability. What they need is orientation. One source of orientation is the shared vision for their project or company. The important thing is that this vision not merely echo your goal – "We want to double our sales" or "We want to be the top supplier of XYZ in the market" are not visions to which your employees can latch on emotionally. A vision is something that is able to resonate with people emotionally and carry the team through turbulent and challenging times, enabling team members to see the tasks before them in ways to which they can relate.

The second source of orientation is shared values. I am not referring here to the cute slogans that companies hang in the hallways for employees to ignore. I am referring to the values that these employees actually experience in the workplace – the values that are reflected in both behavior and communication. Underlying values provide a reliable foundation to guide people within a system regarding how to act. They make control unnecessary, because people's behavior is already conditioned by these values. Within this framework, things can also be tested and, if they fail, rejected. Confusion is limited by the fact that employees have a basic sense of orientation.

"If you desire to see, learn how to act."
HEINZ VON FOERSTER

Leadership is understanding and assessing

The increased complexity of our world has meant the beginning of a change in what it means to lead and manage. This change will have to continue in order for organizations to continue to be successful in the future. So what exactly are the duties of managers now? If you are expecting a simple recipe like "12 key ingredients for success" here, then you are going to be disappointed – there are no more recipes or formulas, no best practices, no predetermined path to success. Nowadays, we need chefs – because chefs know how to improvise, adapting how they will proceed depending upon the situation. They have experience, and they put it to use. They do not try to fight against the conditions with which they are presented, but rather make use of whatever is available to them. Instead of becoming victims of complexity, they have mastered it.

 The question is not "How can I manage a complex organization?", but rather "How can I manage *in* a complex organization?"

Managers are just as much a part of a system as their employees. There is no such thing as managing from the outside or managing from above. The classic image of management that people have in their heads needs an update – the old notion of having comprehensive knowledge, complete understanding, and absolute control is obsolete. And a manager's task has changed as well – nowadays, it is all about understanding and assessing the system.

The manager who understands and assesses a system:

➤ is able to withstand complexity
➤ recognizes interrelationships and patterns
➤ utilizes his knowledge in order to give stimuli and generate resonance
➤ assesses the system's behavior and utilizes feedback to regulate it
➤ creates the right framework and space to allow interconnectedness
➤ takes advantage of the collective intuition and intelligence

SUMMING UP:

- ❖ **Control is an important force that drives people's actions.**
- ❖ **Complex situations cannot be controlled.**
- ❖ **We all want to be heroes, but the old type of hero is not what is needed nowadays.**
- ❖ **Complexity is a challenge that we have to face – it can be regulated, but not controlled.**
- ❖ **Understanding and assessing the system are a manager's main tasks**

Misconception #8:
Competition is good
for business

Yes, I admit it – I'm a channel-surfer. And while zapping around, I get a quick look at many of the different game shows, reality shows, documentary shows, etc., that flicker into our living rooms each day. I watch obese people doing physical challenges. I see Z-list celebrities locking horns while locked up in a house together. Then there are the mixed teams of celebs and "regular" people who answer trivia questions and perform a variety of tasks. And last but not least, the contestants who race across the globe participating in all sorts of silly challenges.

And the one thing that all of these shows have in common? Competition. Who can lose more weight, who knows more, who can endure more, who can jump higher, who can dive deeper. And we love watching it all, don't we?

They say that "competition is good for business". Yes, it may be true that contestants persevere more or lose more weight when they are motivated to avoid last place in a group. It may be true that people achieve more under such conditions than they would all alone in their own homes. And yes, it may even be true that the contestants in these shows transcend limits – the only question is whether they are the limits of the contestants' abilities or just the limits of good taste. What is actually gained from all this?

In all of these competitions, there is one thing missing – the market. Such competitions contribute nothing to the common good and do nothing to benefit any circumstances beyond the half-life of the show. They are about nothing more than achieving individual goals. That's fine, you may argue, because such competition resembles that of the sports world – not the competition of the business world. And that makes sense. The sticking point, however, is that we tend to transfer the thinking from such competitions directly to our organizations – i.e., the idea that competition results in more performance, ideas, and innovation.

This is basically a mantra of many managers – and they truly believe that "internal competition" ensures that their employees will come up with their best ideas and will always be ready to take it up a notch. The sales department is always at the front of their minds here. It is assumed that salespeople – and especially sales managers – are basically aggressive alpha males (they don't talk much about the saleswomen) who just can't get enough friendly competition.

Points are awarded, just like in any good game show – except that here they're called "key performance indicators" (KPIs), and the game format is "incentive system". Game shows and sales departments basically follow the same premise – participants earn money based on their results in achieving clearly defined performance thresholds.

Or do you find this comparison far-fetched? Ultimately, people do differentiate in their minds between what they see on TV and what they experience in reality – but nevertheless, their actual behavior and the mechanisms behind it are very much comparable to what we see in these shows. Promoting competition with an incentivization scheme leads individuals to "optimize" their own sphere. Salespeople make sure that they sell more of the products that will earn them higher commissions. And they "guard" their customers like treasure, limiting the information that they are willing to share. Getting their KPIs as high as possible becomes their main goal. Meanwhile, they ignore the fact that achieving particular indicators can never actually represent a company goal. Competition and the silo mentality become automatic. The system is self-organized – and if competition is a "constraint", then the employees will behave accordingly and compete with each other. This is detrimental to the organization and its overarching goals. In the long run, it will be driven in the wrong direction.

Competition drives more competition, at least where there is no market in play. In the long run, however, it is not what will generate the best ideas and innovations – it will simply get you the best competitors. When watching one of those TV shows, have you ever wondered what the contestants could achieve if they were to cooperate instead of competing? This is a crucial question in real life – especially when matters become complex.

Is competition in our blood?

Competition seems to be everywhere, right? Not a day passes during which we don't find ourselves in competition with somebody over something. We want the parking spot closest to the door. We want to get at the front of the line in the cafeteria. We don't want the other department to have more time than us at the meeting. We don't want our new colleague to be earning more than us. Wherever you look, there is always competition happening. Especially in our own minds, in which there are at least two places where we see competition as being vital: nature and the market economy. It's right there in the name – the very word "market" implies competition. However, we often promote competition even where there is no market in play – and the question is why we do so. Is there no other way?

There is a stubbornly persistent belief in our minds that evolution basically comes about as a result of competition – the idea is that only competition leads to natural selection, which is what brings out "the best". Most people grow up with this basic idea and continuously find it confirmed in life, because they constantly have to compete – for their parents' attention, for good marks in school, for a place on the football team, and so on. This, however, does not result in evolution – at most, it results in elimination.

 When there is competition for the same thing, someone eventually has to lose. Everyone cannot be a winner.

Let's stick with nature for a moment, as a model for "meaningful" competition. There is always competition in nature, both between species and within each species. There is competition, for example, for food and for mates, this latter serving the very important function of preserving the species. When a dog urinates on something, he is marking the territory where the food and the females "belong" to him.

This sort of territorial behavior can be found in the business world too. Managers in particular sometimes mark their territory quite conspicuously. This can be seen, for example, in competition regarding office size and furnishings, company cars, and seats at the conference table – where the "top dog" occupies lots of physical space, perhaps even using several chairs to further mark his territory. But what is all this competition about? Presumably, at the workplace, it is not about food and mates (although even this cannot always be ruled out). Rather, it is about recognition, power, money, career advancement, and status. This can take on quite grotesque forms, with people essentially competing over who can get more stressed out – each trying to outdo the others and show that they can work longer and harder and put in the most overtime hours.

This sort of competition certainly does not produce innovations, new ideas, or efficiencies. Rather, they turn individuals into walnut trees. How so? Walnut trees secrete chemical substances into the ground that inhibit the growth of other species, so unwanted competitors cannot even take root below them – only nettles end up growing there.

 The belief that life is all about competition is still deeply rooted inside us.

So we act accordingly and notice that everyone else is doing the same. It's not for nothing that we speak of the "rat race" and of "big fish" vs. "small fish".

Is competition just in our blood? Yes, it is – although it is not the only approach at our disposal. Yet we still keep sticking to the belief that this is the case – and unfortunately see ample supporting evidence in our daily lives, which makes it difficult for us to turn away from the purely competitive approach. Nature, however, also provides wonderful examples showing us that cooperation makes sense too – and that it pays off not only for the collective, but also for each individual. So, what is the significance of competition vs. cooperation when it comes to dealing with complexity?

Competition or cooperation?

You, as a manager, are facing a complex problem that you are unable to solve. So you decide to do something that seems totally natural – you have two of your best employees each work on the matter, and then come back to you with the best ideas they have. The thinking is that this competition will make both of them highly motivated to give it their all and thus find the best possible solutions.

If this happens in an environment where there is trust and openness, then it may be able to work well. Unfortunately, however, it is often the case that the two experts do not even know that they are in competition, or the competition is linked to individual goals and incentives. This basically minimizes the chances of a fruitful competition. Moreover, in a complex context, such an idea is actually counterproductive – it promotes both selfish communication behavior and the silo mentality, which are completely incompatible with mastering complexity. Even experts cannot fully grasp complex problems, because complexity exceeds the limits of the cognitive abilities of individuals – so what we need is the collective intelligence.

 Complexity always means interconnectedness. More interconnectedness, in turn, means more complexity and thus more non-linearity.

Let's recall the basic idea of Ashby's Law: complex problems require complex answers. So, what we need is just the opposite of the silo mentality and the dog-eat-dog attitude. We need cooperation – and we are, in fact, cut out for this just as much as we are for competition.

Cooperation means trust

Every day, companies and unions negotiate with each other. Since 2014, Lufthansa and the pilots' union Cockpit have been at it regarding a so-called "transitional pension" scheme that affects 5,400 pilots. At present, the pilots may enter into retirement as early as 55 years old; they do so at an average age of 59; Lufthansa, however, considers this unsustainable and wants to set the pensionable age limit at 61. Tough discussions have dragged on over several months, with intermittent strikes. Spokespeople from the employer's side report that the union had planned the strike even before the negotiations were held.

The union publicly labels these claims outrageous, saying that Lufthansa is only interested in increasing its profits at the expense of its employees. Before the next round of negotiations, it will seek its members' approval for a labor dispute, and will deliberate over whether it will carry out further discussions or just immediately go on strike again. Broadly speaking, this is where the negotiating parties stand. Even looking at the situation from the outside, without knowing the nitty-gritty details of the discussions, it is clear what is lacking in this whole debate: trust. Both sides mistrust each other, which leads to positions becoming entrenched and arguments giving way to threats. Cooperation becomes very difficult under such circumstances. Such debates usually end in either a ceasefire or an uneasy compromise under which one side emerges as a clear loser.

The Lufthansa case is just one example of continuously failing negotiations that are characterized by a lack of trust. When trust is lacking, cooperation will be lacking as well – and the parties will just fight, instead of finding solutions. So what can be done in order to reach a cooperative solution? Do such interactions always have to be hard fought? Is there some strategy by which both parties can emerge as winners? And what do we need in order to be able to start trusting and cooperating?

Our answers will come from researchers Robert Axelrod and Paul Zak, whose experiments and studies have produced astonishing results. Let's take a look at them – one at a time.

Tit for tat

It was Robert Axelrod's book "The Evolution of Cooperation" (2009) that popularized the idea of the "tit-for-tat" strategy (➡ Glossary). In this book, Axelrod showed how cooperation could be achieved even where each party would choose selfish behavior in the short term. The "prisoner's dilemma", an essential part of game theory, was used as the starting point for his analysis. In this zero-sum game, two participants must make decisions while unable to communicate with each other. In the classic variant, they are criminals who have been caught after a bank robbery. There is not enough evidence to prosecute them for the robbery, but each can be sentenced to three years in prison for illegal weapons possession.

The prosecutor tells each of them the following: "Look, we are going to prosecute you for illegal weapons possession, which means at least three years in prison. But I'm going to offer you a deal. If your accomplice keeps quiet and you confess to the robbery, then you can go free and your accomplice will spend ten years in prison. On other hand, though, if you keep quiet and your accomplice confesses to the robbery, then he will go free and you will spend ten years in prison. If you both confess, then you will each spend five years in prison." The criminals are thus presented with the following possibilities:

	Prisoner B keeps quiet	Prisoner B confesses
Prisoner A keeps quiet	Both spend 3 years in prison.	B goes free. A spends 10 years in prison.
Prisoner A confesses	A goes free. B spends 10 years in prison.	Both spend 5 years in prison.

Each of the criminals has a clear incentive to confess ("defect" in game theory terminology), no matter what the other does. In the event the other keeps quiet, it is better to confess and go free than to keep quiet and spend three years in prison. And in the event the other confesses, it is better to confess and spend five years in prison than to keep quiet and be sentenced to ten years. So if the two joined forces only for the robbery and don't intend to establish any further connection, then the most "rational" strategy for each one is to confess (i.e., defect) – and thus each criminal trying to extract the greatest advantage for himself will end up leading to both criminals spending five years in prison. A true win-win situation would only be achieved if both criminals were to keep quiet – and thus spend only three years in prison. But this would require cooperation, which in turn requires trust.

 The less two competing people know each other, the less consideration they will have for each other.

This can often be seen, for example, in our one-off interactions with others in traffic or when competing for a good parking spot. In our working environments, however, we interact with each other again and again – and this changes the game.

What does it look like in your organization? Are the framework conditions geared towards cooperation or competition?

	Yes	No
Interdepartmental interactions happen on the basis of mutual respect.		
Different teams are interconnected.		
Team sizes are conducive to intra-team coordination.		
Exchanging information and staying in contact are seen as desirable and are encouraged.		
Trust is given in advance.		
Cooperation pays off (in terms of reputation, time, etc.)		
Competitive rivalries are frowned upon.		

If you can answer "yes" to most of these, then you are well on your way to having an organization in which cooperation flourishes.

In the prisoner's dilemma, as described above, there is only one "round" of play. It represents decision-making in one-off interactions – there is no reason for us to consider others, for example, when trying to get the best parking spot at the supermarket or the best seat on the train. You will never see these people again, and so you can focus on advancing your own interests in good conscience. Robert Axelrod's research, however, assumed that we live and work with others whom we encounter repeatedly. What might change, then, if we were to take the same train every morning and board with the same people? What strategy is now the best – and might it make a difference with regard to whether we defect or cooperate?

To answer this, Axelrod turned to the iterated prisoner's dilemma. He wrote a simple computer program, for which he asked a variety of experts to develop strategies that would play iterated instances of the game opposite each other. Many peers from the fields of mathematics, computer science, and psychology submitted a wide range of strategies. The one that emerged as the most successful was the "tit-for-tat" strategy, submitted by Anatol Rapoport, which followed a simple pattern: Each criminal started off by cooperating – and from then on, simply repeated his counterpart's action from the previous round. While "rational" strategies eventually cannibalized themselves, and the practitioner of the tit-for-tat strategy did not always come out better than his counterpart, this was ultimately the strategy that most facilitated good cooperation between the two sides.

"Tit for tat!"

Axelrod revealed that a good-natured tit-for-tat strategy was stable over the medium and long term in an environment characterized by competition. There was, however, one snag: Tit-for-tat is prone to errors in real life, because people don't always act like computer programs. If a person were to mistakenly defect instead of cooperating, Rapoport's strategy would respond by defecting and this cycle would then repeat itself endlessly. In real life, the so-called "tit-for-two-tats" strategy is even better. Under this strategy, one only defects after one's counterpart has defected *twice*. This is more forgiving, because it excuses the occasional mistake.

The strategy that we choose to use in the hustle and bustle of our organizations is dependent upon many factors, including the particular context.

 But one thing is certain: Cooperation requires trust.

If trust is lacking, then people will probably rather choose a selfish path. Wouldn't it be great, then, if there were some mechanism by which trust could just be switched on or off? Well, there is.

No trust without oxytocin

Is there actually a molecule that affects our morality? Neuroeconomist Paul Zak has studied this question intensively, and he says that the answer is yes – and its name is oxytocin. Oxytocin is produced in both our blood and our brain, although it is only released in small quantities. And it is highly volatile, with a half-life period of about three minutes at room temperature. After believing that he had identified oxytocin as the neurotransmitter that is responsible for our morality, Zak began an extensive series of tests.

First, to test how oxytocin relates to trustworthiness, a large number of test subjects were brought to a laboratory to have their oxytocin levels measured before and after the following experiment. Each test subject A was given ten dollars, and was asked if they were willing to send some or all of this amount to an unknown test subject B. B would then receive triple the amount sent by A. None of the test subjects could see or communicate with their counterparts, but A knew that B would have the option of keeping all of the money or sending some of it back. Each A thus had to decide: Can I trust that the person to whom I send money will send some of it back? If this trust was lacking, then it would be better for A to just keep the full ten dollars. It turned out that the more money A received and gave away, the higher his or her oxytocin levels were.

This experiment was carried out several times around the world, and the research was in agreement – the first transaction (sending money) gauged trust, and the second (returning money) gauged trustworthiness. But Paul Zak was not yet satisfied. Other molecules measured in the test subjects were correlated with the oxytocin – so he sought a way to affect the oxytocin in the brain directly. And he found it in the form of a nasal inhaler. Another group of 200 test subjects was gathered, and the experiment was carried out once again, with each subject inhaling either oxytocin or a placebo. Of those who had received oxytocin, twice as many actually sent all ten dollars to the unknown recipient. According to Zak's findings, oxytocin increases our trust in others. It increases our empathy.

The basic message here is that we are not only capable of cooperating, but rather actually tend towards cooperation instead of competition, at least as long as a commensurate amount of oxytocin is present in our bodies. The other side of the coin, however, is that stress inhibits the production of oxytocin, and thus makes us less empathetic – so when we are under pressure, we tend to be distrustful and wary. This is something that must be considered if you work in a high-pressure environment and want to "order" your employees to cooperate. This will be difficult for them, and they may need lots of assistance. In difficult, somewhat gridlocked negotiations such as those between Lufthansa and the pilots' union, it might come down to equipping the conference room with oxytocin inhalers.

How to build and keep trust in the workplace:

➤ *Practice what you preach.*
Be true to your words, and do as you tell others to do. Even when you will be unable to stick to your word, be transparent about it.

➤ *Give trust to get trust*
As a manager, it is up to you to create a stock of trust with your employees. Cooperation must be initiated by you.

➤ *Set an example*
Be aware that your staff members are watching how you interact with other departments, coworkers, and representatives from other companies, and are monitoring your trustworthiness.

➤ *Establish transparency*
Brief your employees early, comprehensively, and with as much detail as possible, even with regard to decisions that are still pending – otherwise, they will automatically just create their own "truths".

➤ *Stick to the truth*
Be honest!

➤ *Be reliable*
Don't keep double standards for yourself and your employees. Your employees should always know where they stand with you.

➤ *Be open*
Impart something of yourself, your thoughts, and your sentiments. Show yourself as a person.

➤ *Demonstrate your competence*
Competence earns trust. Take advantage of this.

➤ *Be willing and able to listen*
Your employees' concerns and thoughts should be in good hands with you. Be interested in what they have to say.

Make cooperation worth it

Is the difference between competition and cooperation basically like the difference between selfishness and self-sacrifice? Is it a question of one or the other? Not at all. Competition does not mean thinking only of oneself, and cooperation does not mean that everyone loves each other. The truth, as usual, lies somewhere in between. When managing in a complex organization, it is important to recognize that competition is not a criterion for success. It is not about setting two linear processes up against each other in order to pump out increases in productivity – rather, it is about finding new ideas and solutions to address complex issues. However, on a daily basis, what many people experience are only power struggles, competitions for resources, people withholding information from others to gain the upper hand, and other such sorts of competitive behavior – so many organizations find themselves stuck with a predicament. Competition often pays off, while cooperation is not explicitly recognized. And this is exactly what needs to be fixed.

> *"Blame is not for failure, it is for failing to help or ask for help."*
> JØRGEN VIG KNUDSTORP, CEO OF THE LEGO GROUP

Morieux and Tollman, in their book *Six Simple Rules: How to Manage Complexity without Getting Complicated* (2014), describe such an adjustment using the example of a railway company. Essential to the success of this company was the on-time arrival of its trains – but it was precisely in this area that performance had worsened significantly in recent years, with the rate of on-time arrivals having dropped below 80 percent. The management team had already launched various initiatives to improve punctuality, such as updating the traffic control system, optimizing cleaning processes, and creating a new function to monitor delays. None of these initiatives were truly successful, as each one resulted in only small improvements in punctuality but was quickly dropped due to other negative effects. It was a typical trial-and-error strategy, which often seeks to shorten, tighten, speed up, or monitor some existing process.

Morieux and his colleagues advised the company management to improve cooperation between employees, instead of relying on individual accountability and just constantly investing more resources. This approach met with disapproval among the employees, especially on the operational level. One maintenance supervisor said, "Lack of cooperation is an excuse. If we are all accountable in our silos, the trains will be on time, cooperation or not. My job is to make sure that the trains leave maintenance in the right way at the right time."

This is just one quote that shows how pronounced the silo mentality and behavior was in this organization. Since they never worked outside their own areas, the employees had no experience with the consequences of their activities. They did not think beyond the limits of their own area. Moreover, the different operational units, such as train drivers, maintenance staff, conductors, and station crew, did not even communicate with each other regarding their work and how much time was necessary for it. If one unit needed more time than planned for their responsibilities, none of the other units were proactively informed about this.

This changed, however, as soon as a crisis arose. In extreme weather conditions, for example, all units immediately established efficient lines of communication and effective feedback loops, working out solutions together. During the regular course of operations, though, they regarded this as unnecessary. So what the management had to do, with Morieux's assistance, was find some inducement that would push the employees to cooperate on a constant basis. While working toward this, they realized that the unit managers did not see their real goal as making sure that trains arrived on time – but rather as avoiding the blame whenever trains got delayed. And, in fact, one of the improvements that had been implemented only exacerbated this – the new monitoring system was configured to identify the responsible unit in the event of delays, and that unit would then be held guilty and saddled with the blame for causing the delay.

 If everyone wants to avoid blame, this will usually just result in them avoiding admitting to errors or (in this case) delays. No one will ask others for help; instead, each area will try to handle its problems on its own, further reinforcing silo behavior.

After intense deliberations, the management of the railway company took a radical step – from then on, guilt and blame would instead fall on the unit that did not cooperate, rather than the unit that was technically at fault. Basically, if Unit A had a problem or needed more time, and asked Unit B for assistance, then Unit B would be held responsible for the delay; if Unit A did not admit to the problem or ask Unit B for assistance, then Unit A would be held responsible. The cooperation principle replaced the causative principle – the question was no longer "who caused the delay?", but rather "who stood in the way of finding a solution?" If it sounds like employees were "ordered" to cooperate, they basically were – but does that mean the new approach met with resistance from the employees? No, quite the contrary. The biggest change was merely that they had to ask for assistance from other units. And this mechanism, based on mutual assistance and cooperation, was immediately adopted and implemented.

Eliminating the silo mentality was certainly no easy task, and there were undoubtedly employees who initially complied due only to pressure, despite their internal reservations. After all, this did require abandoning ingrained patterns of behavior – internal attitudes do not change overnight, but rather only over time. Ultimately, however, this example makes clear that, when it comes to complex tasks, cooperation is much more promising than competition and isolated thinking. Cooperation is a necessity in complex systems.

Four months after the company implemented this major change on their most important lines, the on-time arrival rate on these lines had climbed to 95 percent. The employees were very happy about the new approach as well, for three main reasons:

> *Customer relations had improved considerably, as employees were now able to provide passengers with better information regarding delays.*
> *Communications between operational units were significantly enhanced, with managers acting as links between the different units.*
> *Employees were proud of being able to break records.*

"If you want to go quickly, go alone. If you want to go far, go together."
AFRICAN PROVERB

The approach chosen by this company is indicative, above all, of transparency. The company asks for cooperation, as a result of which mistakes and uncertainties are made transparent. It only works when these mistakes do not automatically lead to blame and punishment. There are thus two essential prerequisites here – trust, and an appropriate manner of dealing with mistakes. It should be clear by now that when it comes to cooperation, we do not speak of processes, but rather of attitudes and perspectives – and changing these takes much longer than changing behavior.

 It is up to you to set an example and orient your employees to the new cooperative approach that you are implementing. Give your employees time to gain experience with it, and put up with their initial reservations or resistance.

Change always means working against the momentum of habit, and this takes time and energy. You will need both of these in order to turn a competitive environment into a cooperative one. Managers usually find it much easier to simply impede cooperation, especially on the levels of processes, structures, and goals.

How to impede cooperation:

➢ Treat your employees only as individuals, while inhibiting the development of a team identity.
➢ Set many different goals within the team.
➢ Create incentive systems that make employees focus on achieving individual goals.
➢ Formulate responsibilities as vaguely as possible and assign each one to several employees.
➢ Do not draw boundaries with regard to tasks, resources, and available time.
➢ Encourage competition for resources.
➢ Keep your staff separated from the rest of the organization.
➢ Find out who made mistakes and punish them publicly.
➢ Inhibit discourse and debate.
➢ Decide EVERYTHING.

SUMMING UP:

❖ **Competition always produces winners and losers.**
❖ **Competition makes sense where there is a market.**
❖ **Competition does not lead to evolution, only elimination.**
❖ **Complex systems are interconnected and have no silos.**
❖ **Cooperation is the bedrock of interconnectedness.**
❖ **Cooperation requires trust, transparency, and discussion.**

Misconception #9:
There needs to be a clear, formal hierarchy

Where do you stand in the hierarchy of your family, of your company, etc.? Are you an alpha or an omega? There are hierarchies everywhere we go, and most of us find this not only normal, but also reasonable. The one at the top of the hierarchy is the one who says what's what, and that's really the way it ought to be. We think hierarchically and we organize ourselves accordingly – and this way, each person's value to an organization is immediately clear. Higher-ranking employees trump lower-ranking employees when it comes to decision-making, and the lower-ranking ones must then obey. It's no coincidence that, in most company buildings, you need to go upstairs in order to meet with the CEO or the board of directors.

We have internalized this notion of the ubiquity and necessity of hierarchies to such an extent that we no longer find anything strange in the plethora of nonsensical metaphors that are presented to us in management literature and seminars. Comparisons from the animal world are especially common – because most species live in hierarchical groups, just like we do. But the comparisons with sheep, wolves, and donkeys really are a bit clumsy. Sure, we're flattered to be compared to a strong, clever animal like the wolf – but did you know that wolves actually live in packs that are familial and supportive, with no fighting over ranks in the hierarchy? Only in captivity do wolves quarrel over their position in the pack – and I presume that captivity is not an image you want to have associated with yourself and your organization.

The wolf makes us think of an alpha animal, a leader, at the top of the food chain. On the other hand, we think of the chicken as being lower in the hierarchy of animals. Chickens, in fact, are often used as examples of how hierarchies always emerge in nature – if a number of chickens are kept together in an enclosure, they will soon establish a "pecking order". This comparison is also useful when it comes to second-in-commands, because there is also a "beta chicken" – who dominates all of the others besides the alpha, of course. That's the way we like it, simple and straightforward. We like finding out whether our personality type is that of the ox, lion, cat, or deer – that is, phlegmatic, sanguine, choleric, or melancholy. Maybe you see yourself in one of these – but let's get back to the issue of hierarchies.

For many years now, I have been using horses in team training sessions. The participants observe the horses, and the first question I usually ask them is, "What do you think – which horse is the boss in this herd?" The responses are always very similar, and can be boiled down to the following: "That grey/brown/multicolored horse is the boss, because he's clearly the one that's ordering the others around."

There it is again – our distinct image of how a team functions. One says what should be done, and the others follow. Hierarchy reigns supreme. But if we were to transfer the actual horse herd structure over to a company, people would be shocked. Horses live in a matriarchy. There is an alpha mare who determines when they will graze, sleep, roam, or flee. She actually is often rather inconspicuous from the outside – but is confident and can keep sight of the big picture. She makes sure that the rowdier horses don't run wild and that a proper atmosphere is maintained.

The "lead stallion", who we like to imagine looking like Black Beauty, is responsible for protecting the herd and making sure stragglers don't fall behind when it's time to run away. Regardless of their rank, horses are extremely perceptive animals; they are also faithful, unbiased, non-calculating, and always in the present. They can see almost a full 360 degrees around them – and oh, how glad I would be if we could transfer this trait over to ourselves and our organizations. But back to the topic.

Wolves, chickens, and horses aren't known for solving complex problems – but some other animals are. Bumblebees, for example, solve the famous "traveling salesman problem" when collecting pollen, with their navigation system enabling them to find the shortest route possible. Brazilian fire ants, by contrast, are faced with the problem of surviving floods – and in order to do so, they hook into each other to form a sort of raft that floats. And there are numerous other such examples. What is especially interesting about these amazing stories is how these bumblebees, ants, etc. organize themselves – they live in colonies, and have no interest at all in a centrally controlled hierarchy.

When we observe a group of animals, we immediately construct a sort of organizational chart in our minds, enabling us to understand their hierarchy and to see the order in their system. But we usually don't even consider the possibility that an organization can be structured in a non-hierarchical way. And this truly is a shame.

Hierarchy – Stormy iron or sacred rule?

For as long as authority has existed, hierarchies have existed as well. The first step towards hierarchization occurred six thousand years ago, when shepherds settled down and started controlling access to resources, fencing off their flocks and denying entry to others. They had no choice but to defend their "territory" with weapons. Some claim that the original meaning of the term "hierarchy" is "stormy iron", with reference to the defense of resources. The more commonly given etymology is "sacred rule", from the Greek *hierós* ("sacred") and *arkhé* ("rule"). This second meaning may have grown out of the first.

We find hierarchies in almost every place where people live or work together in groups. In the hierarchy of ancient Egypt, for example, the pharaoh had absolute power, controlling political life and owning all the land in his kingdom. Below him were the vizier, the highest-ranking advisors, and the high priests, followed by other officials and scribes. In the Catholic Church, the Pope is at the top of the hierarchy as the "Holy Father". Subordinate to him are the various church officials and dignitaries at their respective ranks, such as cardinals, bishops, deacons, parish priests, and chaplains. Likewise, in the armed forces, a soldier's rank tells us where he or she stands in the hierarchy; climbing upwards may be possible. We find a pyramid-shaped structure in many forms of government – but in any case, there are always superior and subordinate powers, regardless of whether the system is based on absolutism, aristocracy, despotism, monarchy, or any other type of rule. Even when it comes to family, some people think in terms of a hierarchical ranking, such as: father, mother, child.

And in our companies too, we are used to hierarchical structures. They seem logical to us, especially when people and their tasks are well aligned and a company goal is to be achieved. When we want to get to know an organization, we immediately ask for a current organizational chart. It "tells" us what the organization is, what it does, and how it functions – or at least that's what we think. This idea is an established dogma that we have internalized – one of several that together ensure that we stick to this model without even questioning it.

Dogmatic beliefs that make us favor hierarchy:

➤ When a company grows, a hierarchical pyramid structure is indispensable.
➤ Fewer conflicts arise in a hierarchy, and those that do are more quickly settled.
➤ The pyramid structure fosters quick decision-making.
➤ Decisions are nearly impossible without hierarchy.
➤ Hierarchy facilitates efficiency.
➤ Hierarchy regulates the flow of information.
➤ Standardization (of tasks, roles, etc.) is necessary and can best be achieved via hierarchical structures.
➤ People need clear, well-defined tasks and responsibilities.
➤ An absence of hierarchy means chaos.

The list of arguments made in favor of hierarchical structures can easily be extended. And so, we believe that a hierarchical organization is sensible or even imperative. Some managers with whom I have worked were not necessarily in favor of hierarchies per se – they just (still) could not see any alternatives, and could not even imagine an organizational form that focused on complexity and system dynamic. Before going into detail about these new forms, I would suggest that you consider your (personal and organizational) dogmatic beliefs regarding hierarchical organizational structures. Reflect upon the following questions (by yourself and with your management team) – they can help you overcome some of the stubborn, outdated dogmatic beliefs.

Whether flat or tall – rigid hierarchies are obsolete

The success story of hierarchical control started in the early 20th century with Frederick Taylor's scientific management. Taylor sought to use a scientific approach to optimize work processes and business management, in order to make prosperity possible for all. His basic assumption was that workers who naturally tend towards sluggishness must be driven towards greater productivity. If the workers' productivity increased, then the company's profits would too, which meant that the workers' wages could be adjusted upwards as well.

The basic principles of scientific management:

➢ Strict separation between tasks to be handled by the management (planning) and workers (executing).
➢ Workers execute based upon instructions specified by the management.
➢ Work is broken up into the smallest possible processes, such that these can be precisely defined.
➢ Skilled workers are no longer necessary to execute tasks.
➢ Money is used to motivate, with wages dependent upon performance.
➢ Analysis of work is to be performed over time.

> *"Hardly a competent workman can be found who does not devote a considerable amount of time to studying just how slowly he can work and still convince his employer that he is going at a good pace."*
> FREDERICK TAYLOR

It was Taylor whose notion of a "functional organization" expanded the classical single-line system in companies like Ford (see also Misconception #7), shortening information paths and leveraging further efficiencies. Ever since then, the typical organizational structure has been a hierarchical pyramid. Back in those days, management sought to use this structure to help with controllability, systemization, precision, certainty, efficiency, and stability. And for the problems and markets of those times, it was a thoroughly successful concept. However, what we often forget when looking at things from our modern-day perspective is that in Fordism (➡ Glossary), for example, mass production was more than an organizational principle. The mass producer had an influence on both the market and society. Nowadays, our post-Fordist competition involves markets that are highly differentiated and products and services that are often customized. The situation today is completely different.

 Companies today are still rooted in, and still regard as "up to date", the essential principles and mindsets via which Taylor and Ford ushered in a new era of management long ago.

Rigid hierarchies are obsolete because:

> **they are unable to respond appropriately to change.** *This is mostly due to the issue of data flow (aka information flow). In order to make decisions, management needs relevant outside information from the environment. However, this contact with the environment does not happen exclusively through management, but rather at many different points in the organization. Key account managers are responsible for client contact, the PR staff deals with the media, purchasers interact with suppliers, and so on. In hierarchical organizations, relevant data must then be sent up the chain, in order to enable management to make decisions and the company to respond to the changing conditions around it. And you all probably know what happens next – before being sent up the chain, the data is processed, summarized, and nicely packaged and filtered. This is done for two reasons. First, because managers only want the data that is necessary and useful – they don't want to have to read a whole novel. And second, because those who are responsible for providing the data try to leverage this role to their advantage. The upshot is that delivering relevant information to decision-makers takes too long and provides them with only a manipulated excerpt of the reality.*

> **they impede interconnectedness.** *The allocation of employees to clearly delineated departments and teams already does not foster communication between them. Each individual work unit gets its own identity, and employees are dedicated first and foremost to their teams. However, in the event of ambiguities or conflicts, the lack of interconnectedness then manifests a clear disadvantage – instead of engaging in discourse with each other, the opposite happens, with employees just passing the problem up the hierarchy and leaving their supervisors to provide clarifications or*

solutions. The employees forget how to reach out to their coworkers themselves and how to stand up for their positions. Instead, the matter just gets escalated, sometimes through several levels of management, until it finally reaches the hierarchical level at which a decision can be made. Those at the top, in turn, often criticize and complain about the whole chain of escalation. But nothing ends up getting changed, because all this escalation naturally also provides for control, information, and a sense of importance.

> **they make conflicting goals inevitable.** *The organization has an overall goal. Within the organization, each department (marketing, IT, finance, sales, etc.) has its own goals and targets to achieve, and these do not clash from the outset – but what do you think drives the individual department heads and other managers? Their own departmental goals, of course, because that's what their bonuses depends on. And this quickly leads to competition between departments, as everyone tries to reach their own goals – at any cost. And even when the conflicting goals are successfully addressed and a mutual solution is found, lots of time and money gets spent in the process.*

> **they foster the silo mentality.** *Obviously, setting different goals and incentivizing different targets encourages people to think and act within the context of their own departments. In hierarchical companies, each group of experts is packed into a separate department. This promotes the silo mentality, directing each person's focus to his own area of specialty and inhibiting interdisciplinary thinking. When it comes to working on projects, this effect is especially seen in the battle for resources and budget allocations.*

> **power and interconnectedness do not go together.** *Interconnectedness is a feature of complex systems. And it is always there, even if many organizations try to impede it. Why this resistance? Because allowing for interconnectedness involves losing power. Power, in the sense of controlling one's employees, does not work anymore in complex organizations – yet many managers still keep trying to exert even more rigorous control. This often results in unused potential, "by-the-book" work, and a loss of trust. Managers are part of the networked system and have an active influence on how its parts interconnect, but they no longer have the power to determine the specific way that they will interconnect.*

> **they designate only the "how" and "what" of an organization, but not the "why".** *The current organizational hierarchy of almost every company can be found in the "About us" section of its website. The thinking behind this is that this hierarchy explains the organization. However, this is not the case. The organizational hierarchy regulates the social relationships in the organization in terms of who is subordinate to whom, and also coordinates how responsibility is allocated for*

different tasks (the "what"). But it does not provide any more information than that. It contains no information about what makes the system tick. What seems more important – and is not made transparent by the hierarchy – is the "why". What does the organization believe in? What do its people believe in? Why do they hold the convictions that they hold?

"No farewell in the world is more difficult than a farewell to power."
CHARLES MAURICE DE TALLEYRAND

But, you may be thinking, *we've been placing great importance on teamwork, communication, and social skills for decades – after all, we don't want employees who work like automatons.* This attitude, however, is not an end in itself. What happened was that management recognized the most glaring disadvantages of organizations with hierarchical control – i.e., inflexibility and information loss – and responded by simply shifting some decision-making to the lower levels of the hierarchy. Involving employees in this manner was supposed to promote the long-scorned sense of self-initiative.

So we try whatever we can to bind individuals to the company. The idea of a corporate identity emerges. But the catch is that we are trying to better utilize employees' potential without actually changing the framework in which they work. The organization and its structures remain the same, but employees are expected to be more committed, contribute ideas, participate in decision-making (at least nominally), collaborate with each other, and communicate "properly". It can't work this way. Some companies have already realized this, but haven't done much about it yet.

 Trying to elicit entrepreneurial thinking from individuals inside a system with hierarchical control does not work.

The disadvantages of a hierarchical pyramid structure have been a subject of discussion for quite some time, as we ponder whether this structure should be left behind. And our world has changed significantly in recent decades, with increased interconnectedness leading to increased complexity and system dynamic. When we combine these factors with the fundamental disadvantages of hierarchical structures, we end up with a clear answer to the question of whether we need new ways of structuring our organizations – and that answer is "yes".

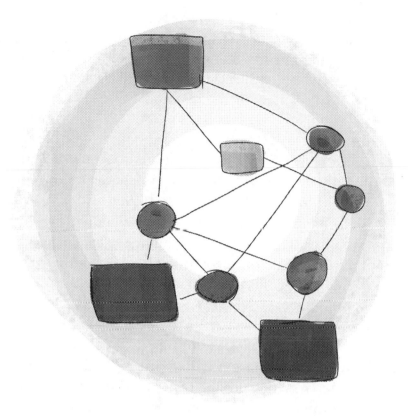

Complex systems are interconnected.

No central control: A path to success

What comes to mind when you think of drugstores? Probably things like "cheap", "price wars", and so on. You may wonder how a drugstore chain with more than 34,000 employees in its 1,400 German branches alone structures itself. Many people believe that they understand the best way to do so: "Well, you need clear processes and guidelines for the branches, distinctly defined roles, and coordinated control of the whole chain from the corporate headquarters." Sure, you can do it that way – if what's most important for you is control.

Götz Werner did things differently – and won the lifetime achievement award of the Deutscher Gründerpreis ("German Founder's Prize") in September 2014 in recognition of his work. In 1973, Werner opened the first "dm drogerie markt" in the center of the city of Karlsruhe. At the time, the path to success was price cuts, self-service, and a simple store layout. However, the following anecdote was supposedly the impetus for Werner to fundamentally rethink his concept of the company: While on a visit to one of his branches in the nineties, Werner leaned on a counter while talking with the branch manager – and it collapsed, breaking the merchandise on the shelf below. The branch manager told him that the counter had needed to be repaired for some time already, but the district manager had simply done nothing about it. In this moment, Werner realized the sorts of ways in which strict hierarchy is inhibitive – and he subsequently launched a comprehensive restructuring process.

dm was changed from a centrally managed company to a decentralized one – responsibility was given to the branches. From then on, they independently determined their own product ranges, work schedules, and salaries. In some cases, supervisors were even chosen by the branch staff. Suggestions for improvement that were received from the branches were implemented by the head office without further inquiry. Trainees, who are dubbed "dm learners" in company parlance, go through a theater workshop in order to work on their self-confidence. There is no longer any organizational chart.

Götz Werner's initiatives were not only focused on his employees, but also on his customers. For example, in 1994, he put an end to promotional pricing in his stores – instead, all dm branches now had prices fixed for all products every four months. And what was the upshot of this radical change of course and clear decentralization? dm left other German drugstore chains in the dust – the company simply performed better.

> "Entrepreneurship means recognizing oneself what is necessary in order to make others take self-initiative."
> GÖTZ WERNER

dm is just one prominent example among a range of companies that have decided, for a variety of reasons, to renounce their organizational charts and their hierarchies of control. Decentralization is a key aspect of this, and the term "networked organization" is often used in this context. I am often asked whether this means that there will no longer be any hierarchy in our companies of the future. The answer is: No *formal* hierarchy that will be visualized in the form of an organizational chart. But there will always be informal hierarchies. At this point, I would like to stress again that we are talking about complex contexts in which centralized, top-down control is inexpedient – however, there will continue to be departments and projects for which centralized control does make sense.

Informal structures, and thus also hierarchies and "leaders", emerge in any company as a result of group dynamic processes. And especially in large organizations, replacing official channels with shorter lines of communication also helps decisions get made and implemented more swiftly.

Especially where an organization is too rigidly structured and stubbornly bureaucratic, informal structures will ensure that it runs better.

Informal structures complement an organization's formal structure, usually filling in the gaps that can develop from either too much or much too little structuring. One even sees informal groups forming their own networks, such as the "old boys' clubs" that exist in many countries. These networks are no less hierarchical than any other organizational structure – so it is wrong to believe that "grassroots democracy" reigns in network organizations. The organizational chart is gone, but hierarchies do still exist.

Replacing the organizational chart with a network

Morning Star is a mid-size California-based company that processes tomatoes. The company has around 400 employees, with the number rising as high as 2,400 in the harvest season. Its products can be found in supermarkets and restaurants across the U.S.A. Business has been going well for many years – especially since the company eliminated its hierarchical pyramid and focused on self-organization. There are no more bosses in this company; instead, employees work together to set their goals in terms of detailed metrics. Even salaries are not determined centrally, but rather by an elected committee. When it comes to purchasing equipment or other items, it is the responsibility of the respective employee to make decisions regarding the amount and necessity of the expenditure. Each employee is fully aware of their shared responsibility for results, and there is complete transparency regarding all costs, processes, and other conditions. All employees have knowledge that usually only managers have – in a way, they are all managers.

> *"You have to be run by ideas, not hierarchies."*
> STEVE JOBS

As an example of a network organization, Morning Star is also cited by consultant Niels Pflaeging in his book *Organize for Complexity* (2014), in which he sketches out a model for network organizations – the "peach" model. The peach pit represents the center of the organization; around it is the periphery. In simplified terms, this network model creates value by having only teams in the periphery interact with the market. Through constant interaction over the long term, they develop market intelligence that leads to new product ideas and innovations. At the same time, the periphery isolates the center from the market, as it is in the center that the ideas and innovations will get implemented – and the energy and focus that is necessary for doing so remains clustered together here.

So who controls such an organization? The answer is obvious: the market. The center has no controlling function – its job is to support and provide. This does not mean that the center is just a tool of the periphery – on the contrary, the two work out together the give and take of each product development or problem to be solved.

It is important to note here underlying the peach model is a flexible understanding of roles. An employee may seize upon an innovative idea while working in a periphery team and later become the person who implements it in the center. The assignment of employees to roles is not rigid, but rather is handled much more flexibly than in many organizations nowadays. Pflaeging believes that there is a "peach" organization hidden inside every traditional pyramidal organization – they are just unable to develop it, due to their hierarchies being too ingrained.

 Nowadays, all organizations are ultimately controlled by the market – but in hierarchical organizations, many managers still try to intervene themselves and take control alongside it.

Decentralization is the crucial aspect of this model – and the lynchpin of network organizations that want to remain flexible and capable of making decisions in complex environments. In addition to dm and Morning Star, this is demonstrated by the many other examples of companies with "new" organizational structures. Extensive information can be found online regarding network organizations such as the automaker Local Motors, the management consultancy Partake, the industrial manufacturer Semco S/A, the hearing aid maker Oticon, and, of course, Toyota.

It is thus not due to a lack of success stories that many companies still do not dare to adapt their organizational design to the increasing complexity of their markets. Rather, it is due firstly to an unwillingness to give up power, and secondly to the fact that such a transformation itself is a highly complex process that cannot be handled via a simple formula, but rather is dependent upon the context of the particular organization. However, it is possible to formulate a few basic first steps, and I will set these out for you below.

First steps towards developing a network organization

- Answer the question: "Is this what we really want?"
- Allow for interconnectedness and strive for discourse about it in management.
- Create transparency, so that your employees can get used to a "management perspective".
- Train your employees in self-management (which they may have forgotten or have never experienced at all).
- Establish the first areas in which your employees can act autonomously.
- Learn how to exercise influence through your contributions, instead of through your power. For this to work, your contributions must be relevant and must generate resonance in your team.

SUMMING UP:

- **We are used to our organizations being designed with hierarchical pyramid structures.**
- **The idea of centralized control as a tool for increasing efficiency comes from the industrial age.**
- **Centralized control, however, is not a suitable tool for dealing with the complex environments of today.**
- **Hierarchical pyramids hinder innovation and value creation.**
- **Interconnectedness means a loss of power.**
- **Network organizations master complexity.**

Mastering Complexity

Mission 4636

The earthquake that struck Haiti on January 12, 2010 was the most severe natural disaster in the country's history. As many as 316,000 were said to have been killed, 300,000 injured, and more than a million left homeless – although the chaos was too great to get reliable numbers, so the figures could only be estimated. The real numbers may have been even higher. The damage to the country's infrastructure, especially in and around its capital Port-au-Prince, was devastating. 70 to 80 percent of the country's emergency call systems had failed, and only mobile radio stations were still working or could at least be repaired quickly. The focus of the immediate relief efforts was on finding and rescuing those who were injured or buried under the rubble. But how could these people – especially those in rural areas – make themselves known? How could they be found?

After hearing of the catastrophe in Haiti, people on several different continents got to work on addressing these questions. Some of them launched initiatives that would come together as Mission 4636 over the span of a few days – and end up saving countless lives. Crowdsourcing made this extraordinary success possible.

The free emergency SMS shortcode 4636

Josh Nesbit, then of the NGO FrontlineSMS, immediately realized that it was crucial for the Haitian people to be able to send and receive information, so he sought some way to create a direct connection to them via radio and telephone. He took advantage of his contacts at the U.S. Department of State, as well as social media such as Twitter and Facebook, to request ideas. One follower from Cameroon suggested that he contact the IP manager of Haiti's largest cellular provider, Digicel. Within 48 hours, the number 4636 was made available as a free, exclusive SMS shortcode.

Now this information had to reach people, and they also needed a way to be able to process all of the text messages they would receive. In order to set up the technical infrastructure for this, the organization InSTEDD flew employees to Haiti, where they had already begun to develop an emergency information system on behalf on the Thomson Reuters Foundation a year before the earthquake. Originally intended to facilitate communication between journalists and victims, the platform was now set up to facilitate the relief effort.

In order to even be able to take advantage of the 4636 system, one "old technology" was indispensable – the radio. Radio was used to inform the population not only about which water and food stations and hospitals were open, but also about the 4636 shortcode. Information quickly spread, and use of the shortcode increased just as quickly. During peak times, 5,000 text messages per hour were processed – and this processing involved much more than simply transferring some bits and bytes.

Bridging the language gap

In order for the incoming text messages to be processed, they needed to be categorized. Josh Nesbit brought computational linguist Rob Munro, with whom he had worked in a similar context in Malawi, on board. Munro became one of the main coordinators over the course of the entire mission, launching many initiatives and addressing the language problem. Knowing that the international relief organizations mostly used English, with Haitian Creole and French being less common, Munro turned to Facebook to find translators both inside and outside Haiti. He soon found himself coordinating several groups of volunteers, with approximately 2,000 translators around the globe contributing to the mission.

Crisis Mapping

Begun by a group of students from Tufts University in Boston, crisis mapping at first happened independently within Mission 4636. The students took advantage of the NGO Ushahidi's platform to use geographical data to create a map of the disaster area, combining Google satellite images with information from tweets and Facebook posts. This platform too had originally been designed for very different purposes, having been developed and used in Africa – but when linked to the SMS and translation platform, it took on crucial significance for Haiti. In the first few days, the focus of the work with Ushahidi was on finding and rescuing the quake victims. Later on, it facilitated a tenfold increase in the speed with which food and medicine was delivered to the population.

These three initiatives within the overall mission were interlinked with each other as well as with the relief organizations. Text messages received via the 4636 shortcode, as well as blog posts and tweets, were stored centrally, reviewed, and translated into English if necessary. Geodata was added or corrected. All of this gave clear indications of where assistance was needed. The relief organizations could also access this data at any time and respond accordingly; this enabled actions to be taken and coordinated, people to be found, food to be delivered, and medical care to be provided. It is difficult to find concrete numbers to measure the success of Mission 4636 in terms of people rescued, but the fact that it was a success is undisputed both inside and outside the participating organizations.

What were the ingredients that made up the mission's success? First, it must be noted that there were several initiatives within the overall project and they were all financed via crowdsourcing, without any central control or coordination. The individual groups that found themselves working together on individual projects were highly specialized and highly interconnected. There were a lot of weak connections and bonds that the participants could make recourse to when needed, in order to compensate for their own lack of know-how – the mission very quickly turned weak bonds into strong ones. Trust was built up rapidly, in part because there was no formal authority that recruited the volunteers – anyone who joined was able to contribute their abilities, knowledge, and connections, and thus participate in the success of the mission.

Weak and strong bonds (➡ Glossary) in social networks

Bonds between people arise through time spent together, emotional closeness, and reciprocal courtesies/services. They can be described as either strong, weak, or non-existent. For a network to function well, both strong and weak bonds are necessary. People who know each other well usually have strong bonds; however, they sometimes tend to seal themselves off from their environment as a group. Weak bonds facilitate the exchange of information and sometimes contribute resources and skills that are otherwise lacking.

Leaders like Robert Munro exemplified what was necessary to the success of Mission 4636 – the will to endure and not give up when difficulties arose. They knew to reinforce positive behavior and quickly and directly provide feedback for successes (and failures). Everyone was thus clear that they had a part in the mission – and a significant one too.

Let's also use this example to take a quick look back at some of the key features of complexity:

Self-organization: There was no central office or "hero" that conceptualized, planned, and implemented Mission 4636. Several different initiatives were launched simultaneously in different places, initially independent of each other. Only over the course of time did the people, initiatives, and organizations become interconnected and networked into a single mission. There were leaders and initiators who made decisions and took actions – but they acted without any intention of controlling anything.

Diversity of factors: The Mission 4636 system consisted of countless initiatives and people, both inside and outside of Haiti – including the Haitian population, the rescue workers, the hospitals, the water suppliers, the students in Boston, the NGOs, and so on. They all kept up (more or less) intensive communication with each other – right in the face of the natural disaster that defined their environment.

Unpredictability: A natural disaster like the earthquake in Haiti goes even beyond complexity and becomes chaotic. Mission 4636 was heavily affected by this, as the entire situation was non-transparent and unpredictable. Even the mission itself was unpredictable, having developed in a self-organized manner from various individual initiatives. The mission's "pattern" emerged only over the course of time.

Variety: The complexity of the mission increased greatly in the span of a few days – and not because lots of people came together to do the same thing, but rather because they each used their own different skills in responding to the different requirements that arose. And there was no headquarters allocating roles and tasks; the system organized itself.

Feedback: Many of the leaders involved in managing the mission were already proficient at feeding back relevant information to employees and others. However, in dealing with the disaster in Haiti, all of the participants in the system transmitted feedback to colleagues and supervisors, whether this feedback consisted of success stories, failures, new requirements, technical conditions, problems, or errors.

Constraints: One constraint that came along with the Haitian population was the language barrier. Most Haitians speak Creole, while most communication in international aid organizations happens in English. Mission 4636 reacted to this constraint by recruiting translators – a prime example of the interrelationship between constraints and a system.

System dynamic: Just like any other complex system, Mission 4636 had its own dynamic. At first, the individual initiatives separately pursued individual goals, such as creating maps or providing information to the Haitian population. They were all doing so for an overarching common goal – helping Haiti through the disaster as well as possible. This common goal enabled them to consolidate their individual goals and even subordinate them where necessary. Side effects and constraints were dealt with, instead of people taking defensive positions. Mission 4636 showed how system dynamic can be harnessed towards success – a key point that many organizations can and should learn from this example.

Of course, there are also critiques to be made of the project. Mistakes were made, some things were not considered, and others were networked together too late. There were some lessons learned with regard to optimization. But still, the mission was a unique and unparalleled global community project that spanned around 50 countries. And I wonder: if Mission 4636 had been planned and managed in our usual manner, how much would it actually have been able to accomplish, and how long would this have taken?

Mission 4636 represents a network-organized success that came about through self-organization rather than rigorous management. Obviously, this example cannot be transferred 1:1 to your organization, where the context is completely different – your organization already exists, and constructing it again from scratch is probably not an option for you. But complexity absolutely can be mastered in existing organizations as well – and there is no organization for which this "does not apply". Although no specific formula can be extrapolated from the example of Mission 4636, it manifests many good suggestions for dealing with complex systems. I will summarize these once again, along with the various issues and considerations discussed over the previous nine chapters, in the following "dos" and "don'ts" for mastering complexity.

What you should stop doing

Chalking success up to methods: We need to put an end to retroactively chalking our successes up to great tools and systematic control – neither can be the singular success factor in complex situations. We are usually very willing to adapt our tools and methods in order to improve, and we are sometimes even willing to pay for outside experts to tell us how things should go – but what we also need is a willingness to challenge our own management philosophy. Where do you stand when it comes to change? Is it "sure, but not me"?

Using the system as an excuse: People throw around the word "system" almost as much as they throw around the word "complexity". When problems arise, they often just say, "It's the system" – with the implicit consequence being, "There's nothing we can do about it." Instead of solutions, this attitude leads to torpor and inaction. In order to change this, we need to make one thing clear: There is no dichotomy between "us" and "the system". We are always a part of the system. We are affected by the system, and we also affect the system. We need to stop shifting responsibility to the system, and instead become aware of the possibilities that we have to influence it.

Thinking only linearly: Looking at the future as a simple continuation of the past is not an adequate way of dealing with time in complex contexts. When planning, we tend to readily carry over assumptions from the past and augment these with a few complementary hypotheses about the future. This is perfectly fine for simple and complicated systems – but in complex systems, management must take place in the present. Decisions should be made, reviewed, revised, and corrected in many short cycles.

Dividing the world into hard and soft factors: The distinction between hard and soft factors is obsolete. In most organizations, two fundamentally different approaches are defined, forming two pillars of management that are each considered separately. The "hard" approach is used in strategy work, requirements management, etc. Born from the idea that changes to structures and processes are what lead to success, the organization's efforts usually only yield changed structures and processes, with success still remaining elusive. On the other hand, we rely upon the "soft" approach when it comes to improving interpersonal relations or managing "emotions". Yet all too often, this manifests itself in purely feel-good, "let's-all-love-each-other" actions that impede cooperation and discourse just as much as the "hard" approach. Neither one of these approaches, in their pure forms, are adequate for dealing with complexity.

Measuring everything against the plan: We need to abandon the expectation of having a long-term plan to predict the future. *But we need to set deadlines for our projects,* you may be thinking. Of course there will still be deadlines – just no straight, linear, pre-planned path to reach them. Planning cycles in complex systems should be short and iterative – this is the only way that we can be flexible in responding to changing conditions. At the same time, we need to practice broadening our field of vision when conceiving possible scenarios for the future, because small actions today may only have great impact much later on.

Training people to pursue individual self-seeking goals: This is just another way of falling into the complexity trap. I do not know of many organizations nowadays that do not use performance indicators and incentivize target figures – however, this makes people focus precisely on these individual aspects in order to achieve their own personal goals, which results in full-fledged silo mentality and behavior. In complex situations, cooperation and improvisation are needed – and this does not work when "the principle" is too important.

Equating symptoms with problems: We need to recognize that symptoms and their underlying problems are two very different things. Project reports get submitted late, departments fail to communicate properly, quarterly sales targets are not met despite favorable market conditions – these are just a few representative examples of situations in which we erroneously tend to equate the symptoms with the actual problems or causes that ultimately lie behind them. We need to stop merely "fixing" such symptoms – and instead start taking a holistic look at the system.

Taking action blindly: When blind action does result in success, it is usually a matter of sheer luck. When we get stuck in the complexity trap, we tend to find it difficult to stay "idle", especially when things are chaotic all around us. What we really need is insight – we need to learn how to understand the system, observing it and recognizing patterns. Our decisions going forward will then have a solid foundation. "Taking action for the sake of taking action" is not effective in complex systems.

Trying to invoke the image of a hero: We need to drop our belief in the "Great Man Theory". All too often, we reduce success to a single cause – the manager / management. And we like to believe that these managers have innate qualities that make them succeed. In complex contexts, however, management is not the sole determinant in the system. It is merely one part of the system. Chalking successes and failures up to the managers' qualities is linear and wrong.

> *"The problem is not the problem. The problem is your attitude about the problem."*
> CAPTAIN JACK SPARROW

What you should do

Think and act "complexly": We need to learn how to start responding to complex problems with complexity. We still usually follow the specific procedure of: (1) Identify the problem, (2) Find the guilty parties (i.e., those who caused the problem), and (3) Order them to fix the problem. And if we notice that the problem is too big for them to fix alone, then we simply put more people on the job – basically, the solution is just "more of the same". However, this linear approach does not work in complex contexts. We first need to recognize and understand the complexity of the problem: what is the system, who are its participants, what interrelationships make up its dynamic, etc. In order to respond in a complex manner, we need cooperation – this is the only way to generate new ideas, innovation, and evolution. The first task of management is thus to create an environment that fosters cooperation.

Recognize patterns: We need to learn how to recognize patterns by observing groups and their interactions. If we only observe individual employees, colleagues, or superiors, then we are blocking out the actual system. Patterns emerge from connections between people, or even from the lack thereof. Simple visualizations can help make the networking patterns apparent. These must then be placed in relation to the problems or tasks being addressed, because achieving goals is ultimately still what matters. Ensuring that employees are interconnected in the "right" way is one of management's most important tasks.

Shift levels: We need to learn to think and manage holistically. We lose sight of the big picture if we only observe the individual elements of the system separately – however, we also cannot master complexity by looking only at the whole. We need to observe both levels concurrently. Constantly shifting between them will allow us to see which individual elements and issues are actually pertinent for the system as a whole. It is not about the individual level or the big picture level alone, but rather about the two of them together and how they relate to each other.

Put guiderails in place: We need to learn to manage people in such a way that they demonstrate behavior that is suitable to complex systems. If we simply train our employees to think in terms of templates ("the way we've always done it"), then we will be unable to find solutions to complex problems in the long run. It is the management's job to create an environment that enables employees to develop their potential and thus grow – and I am certain that there are no employees for whom this "won't work". However, it can never happen without a working relationship that is based on trust and openness. Create the right framework for this.

"Suppose…": We need to learn to work with hypotheses. The difference between a hypothesis and a truth lies in their solidity. A hypothesis is a conjecture about something, which can be adapted, rejected, or corrected at any time. On the other hand, a truth is a (subjective) description of what something is, including causes and effects. In management, we still tend to work much more with truths ("that's the way it is") than with hypotheses ("we presume that's the way it is"). Complex systems cannot be predicted or fully grasped – accordingly, it makes sense for us to work more flexibly with hypotheses, in order to develop the best possible view of future developments.

Foster diversity: We need to manage in a multiperspectival and diverse manner. There is no *single* correct perspective of the world, of a problem, or of a situation. Complex circumstances can only be rendered more accessible (usually retrospectively) by taking different perspectives into account. These perspectives should be different with regard to skills, specializations, and viewpoints. Having teams that are diverse – in the truest sense of the world – is a fundamental prerequisite for being able to generate solutions to complex problems. And merely putting together different people with different skills is not enough – as a manager, you must allow the diversity to manifest itself in the form of discourse and differences.

Think about what could happen: We need to practice thinking about scenarios. Whether we are planning for an upcoming fiscal year, product launch, or project, we are picturing the future. We take this image as the truth, and use risk management to deal with possible stumbling blocks along the way. However, the future cannot be predicted and is not a constant. To account for this, we should start working with scenarios. How *else* might the future look? What other issues may become relevant in the (planned) future? What may become irrelevant? What do the absolute "best-case" and "worst-case" futures look like? These sorts of mental experiments can help you expand your repertoire of solution ideas for the different scenarios – and this increases the number of action options that have at least been considered, in the event that circumstances end up changing.

As a rule: We need to learn to manage "in context". One of the reasons why there are no formulas or recipe books for dealing with complexity is the issue of context. Every symptom, every problem, every situation, and every task must be considered in its own unique context. What worked before or what worked for others will not necessarily result in success for us now. Even the behavior of individuals only tells you something if you look at the context in which they are acting. Forget about quick diagnoses and generalizations – complexity is all about context.

And on a personal level: The following qualities and skills will help you personally deal with complexity and successfully master it:

> ➢ *Courage – to try new things and make mistakes in the process*
> ➢ *Perseverance – because effects often only manifest themselves later on*
> ➢ *Letting go of power – to allow for interconnectedness and self-organization*
> ➢ *A tolerance for uncertainty*
> ➢ *Self-reflection, self-reflection, self-reflection…*

The answer to complexity

What does one call the form of management that successfully masters dealing with complexity? It needs a name – and I call it "holistic management" (➡ Glossary). This type of management does not only regard a system as a collection of individual parts, but rather as a whole. Meanwhile, the individual parts themselves are not dismissed, but rather are taken into consideration as well on another level. Yet the system still always functions as a whole, and cannot be understood or defined merely as the sum of its parts. Holistic management is not a new style or a new method – rather, I see it as a bundle of attitudes, skills, and competencies. You have just read an entire book about it, so at this point I will keep the definition short.

Holistic management

> ➤ takes relationships and contexts into account.
> ➤ works on both the micro (individual) and macro (system) levels at the same time.
> ➤ varies the scaling with which matters are considered and chooses the appropriate cross-section.
> ➤ varies the perspectives from which matters are considered and takes up alternate positions.
> ➤ creates complete transparency for everyone.
> ➤ makes change possible.
> ➤ consistently strikes a balance between structure and flexibility.

Having reached the end of this book, you have hopefully broadened and updated your understanding of complexity and its implications. I hope that you were able to clear up some misconceptions and that you have taken away some valuable stimuli for your work as a manager and a leader. One final question remains: Do we really need a new management approach? My answer is simple: Yes. Yes, because our usual methods no longer suffice. Yes, because our usual way of thinking is not conducive to complex situations. Yes, because we are confronted with different challenges than we were even just a few decades ago. One thing is certain: The world has changed – now it's our turn!

So, on that note: Stay successful!

Appendix

Glossary

Adaptation
In evolutionary terms, adaptation refers to an organism adjusting itself to its environment by developing features and behavioral traits that have the purpose of helping it survive.

Adaptive System
An adaptive system responds to changes and disturbances without losing its integrity. It responds in a flexible way, adapting itself to the changing conditions, without losing sight of goals and results. An adaptive system learns.

Agile Methodology
Originally developed primarily in the field of software development, "agile thinking" methods have been expanding more and more beyond IT. Scrum is the most popular example, but what all of the various agile methods have in common is that they depart from classical linear planning and the conventional understanding of roles.

Bonds (in social networks)
In social networks, there are both strong and weak bonds between the participants. We have strong bonds with those whom we know well and with whom we share common experiences. We may have weak bonds with those whom we know only through the social network and share only a common interest. Both types are important. Strong bonds bear most of the weight, as these are where trust and affinity exist. When necessary, however, we can also quickly access our weak bonds and even take advantage of the others' strong bonds.

Chaos
In chaotic contexts, there are no longer any cause-and-effect relationships, not even in retrospect. What matters when there is chaos is restoring system stability, for which a charismatic or even dictatorial management personality is necessary.

Complexity

Complexity is defined (for the purposes of this book) by the number of factors (participants) in a system and by their reciprocal relationships. The degree of complexity in a system is determined by these two aspects – i.e., the more participants there are and the more they are interconnected, the greater the degree of complexity in the system.

Complicated

Complicated contexts are characterized by clear cause-and-effect relationships and are thus predictable. There can be several possible right solutions. This is the realm of experts, as complicated problems can be solved via analysis.

Confirmation Bias

When we are presented with new information, we tend to match it up against our existing knowledge and look for confirmation, while we subconsciously block out information that contradicts our preexisting expectations.

Constraints

Even complex systems operate within a framework and are subject to constraints. These constraints both affect the system and are affected by the system. The unwritten rules within an organization, for example, serve as constraints.

Disorder

Complex and chaotic systems belong to the "disorderly" world – clear cause-and-effect relationships cannot be discerned a priori.

Diversity

Diversity is absolutely essential in complex systems. A variety of different skills, opinions, perspectives, and knowledge ensures that there will be discourse and disturbances – which allow innovation to take place and new ideas and solutions to be found.

Dynamic

The interconnectedness of a system gives rise to constant change and time pressures. The factors act on each other, such that the system continuously evolves. The system waits for nothing.

Exaptation

Innovations often arise from using something for purposes other than originally intended, rather than from an actual attempt to improve something existent. For example, it is assumed that birds' wings originally evolved solely for thermoregulatory purposes. Once they reached a certain size, though, they were well suited for flapping. An exaptation (for flapping) followed – and later came an adaptation for actual flight.

Fail-safe

Under a fail-safe approach, systems are putatively designed to be failure-proof. In the event of a failure, nothing should impede the exercise of functions or the achievement of goals. This idea has led to many organizations and projects being managed with zero error tolerance, as supposedly everything has been considered and all problems staved off. This can also be seen in how they "test" for solutions in complex contexts – with thinking that remains linear, as they only test out what is most likely to be successful.

Feedback

Feedback is *the* regulation mechanism in complex systems. In order to act successfully as a manager, we must entrench feedback on all levels – professional, procedural, interpersonal, and organizational.

Fordism

Industrialist Henry Ford was among the most famous "early implementers" of the mass production of consumer goods via division of labor, performance agreements, and monetary incentive systems. He applied Taylor's scientific management approach to automobile production – not only maximizing his own production and sales figures, but also influencing the social development of his time.

Groupthink

When in groups, we tend to adapt our opinion to the (anticipated) group opinion. Thus, groups may actually end up making worse decisions than competent individuals.

Heuristics

We are always working with limited knowledge and under time pressures; we thus interpret and assume things in order to be able to make decisions.

Holistic Management

The following are key aspects of a holistic approach to management:

> *Systemic thinking and managing*
> *Considering both the micro and macro levels of the system at all times*
> *Employees in the system can develop their potential*
> *Changes are possible*

Standing behind this is a particular attitude towards both the individuals and the organization (along with its purpose) – an attitude based on respect, courage, curiosity, enthusiasm, a desire to learn, and a willingness to experiment.

Information
Data becomes information only when it produces some meaning for a person.

Information deficit
The most common symptom among managers and executives in complex systems is the subjective sense of an information deficit. This is usually due to having an abundance of data but a lack of relevant information.

Interconnectedness
A system in which interrelationships exist between participants is interconnected.

Interdependence
There are dependencies between the parts or participants in a system. It is important to recognize which parts of the system are existential and what happens when parts are removed.

Locus of control
Having an *internal* locus of control means believing that one can control something (a situation, a team, etc.). Alongside self-efficacy, this plays an important role in motivating us to action. On the other hand, having an *external* locus of control means feeling like something is "out of our control", in which case we will often end up failing to act.

Network organization
A network organization is characterized by its participants acting autonomously, while at the same time sharing common goals and being highly networked and interconnected. The management's main focus is on the interactions within the system, rather than on the individuals.

Non-linearity
The most popular example of non-linearity is the "butterfly effect". A butterfly beating its wings in China can set off a hurricane in America – and likewise, small deviations in the initial conditions of a system can end up having major effects over time.

Non-transparency
In a complex system, the participants and their web of interrelationships cannot be fully grasped. We can only observe excerpts and cross-sections of the system.

With many sections of the system remaining outside our comprehension, the result is non-transparency.

Objectivity

Objectivity is a myth. All information and perceptions are colored by our own personal experiences, knowledge, attitudes, and expectations.

Order

In complex systems, patterns emerge in and through interactions – an order emerges eventually through the implicit constraints.

Relevance

All managers should constantly be questioning the meaning of information, behavior, etc. – including their own. We are naturally quite good at recognizing relevance, but we have developed the tendency to bury it beneath tons of data.

Safe-fail

A safe-fail approach assumes that errors will happen and that this cannot be avoided; the design of the system is thus predicated upon being ready for anything. Experimenting in complex systems means that some of our experiments must fail – otherwise, we will never come to know our limits.

Scientific management

See Taylorism.

Scrum

Scrum is a framework that has its origin in the field of software development. It does not define a procedural model, but rather roles, activities, and artefacts (documents) that facilitate working in a flexible manner. Iterations, regular feedback loops, and lots of discourse enable the organization to respond quickly to changing conditions.

Self-organization

All complex systems are self-organized. They change their structures and generate new patterns, even without any influence from outside. With regard to managing in complex systems, the key aspects are discipline and a suitable set of rules. Constraints (i.e., rules) affect behavior and are also affected by behavior. In order to be successful in social systems, discipline is necessary when dealing with constraints.

Self-efficacy

If we believe that we can perform suitably in a specific situation, then we have an expectation of self-efficacy. We more readily participate in things if we believe that we can accomplish something personally.

Scaling

In complex situations, it is essential to observe the right cross-sections and the different levels together. The thinking and behavior of individuals only makes sense when viewed in the context of the whole.

Simple

In a simple context, the cause-and-effect relationship is clear to all. It is repeatable and transparent.

Stability

Every system strives to achieve a stable state – and seeks stability again after changes and disturbances. It is the responsibility of every manager to ensure the right balance between disturbances to the system and (brief) periods of stability. Instable conditions make change possible and serve as a breeding ground for creativity.

System

An "entity" containing task-, goal-, or purpose-bound participants that interact with each other and are interconnected. Within every organization are many individual systems, which sometimes draw their boundaries differently. These boundaries define what "belongs" to each system and what lies "outside" it. In this book, we are always speaking of open systems that exchange (information, resources, etc.) with their environments.

System dynamics

Interconnectedness and dynamics ensure constant change in a complex system. One can only get to know and understand the system itself through its dynamics, which involve interrelationships and not simple cause-and-effect chains.

Taylorism

Frederick Winslow Taylor's "scientific management" approach involved taking control over work processes with the goal of increasing efficiency. Work steps were to be broken down as much as possible, schedules were to be predetermined, communication was to be defined unidirectionally, and rigorous controls were to be implemented.

Testing

Testing or experimentation is the decision-making mechanism that is to be used in complex contexts. Since the behavior of the system cannot be predicted, we need to test out which impetuses will generate the desired resonance.

Tit for tat

This strategy has its origins in game theory. It demonstrates how cooperation can come about even where selfish behavior pays off for an individual in the short term.

Unpredictability

Complex systems are non-linear. This means that even small actions can have significant effects that may only manifest themselves much later on – which makes such systems impossible to predict. Only in retrospect can clear cause-and-effect relationships (sometimes, though not always) be described.

Variety

Variety refers to the different possible states that a system may take on.

Bibliography

Axelrod, Robert. *The Evolution of Cooperation*. New York: Basic Books, 2006

Bar-Yam, Yaneer. *Making Things Work: Solving Complex Problems in a Complex World*. Cambridge: Knowledge Press, 2004

Beer, Stafford. *Diagnosing the system for organisations*. Hoboken: Wiley, 1995

Binswanger, Mathias. *Sinnlose Wettbewerbe: Warum wir immer mehr Unsinn produzieren*. Freiburg im Breisgau: Herder Verlag, 2012

Borgert, Stephanie. *Resilienz im Projektmanagement: Bitte anschnallen, Turbulenzen! Erfolgskonzepte adaptiver Projekte*. Heidelberg: Springer Gabler, 2013

Brandes, Dieter, and Brandes, Nils. *Einfach managen: Komplexität vermeiden, reduzieren und beherrschen*. Munich: Redline Verlag, 2013

Buche, Antje, Jungbauer-Gans, Monika, Niebuhr, Annekatrin, and Peters, Cornelius. "Diversität und Erfolg von Organisationen." *Zeitschrift für Soziologie*, Vol. 42, No. 6, December 2013, p. 483-501

Coffman, Bryan S. "Weak Signal Research." 1997. Retrieved September 13, 2014, from http://www.mgtaylor.com/mgtaylor/jotm/winter97/wsrintro.htm

Dany, Hans-Christian. *Morgen werde ich Idiot. Kybernetik und Kontrollgesellschaft*. Hamburg: Nautilus, 2013

Dobelli, Rolf. *Die Kunst des klaren Denkens: 52 Denkfehler, die Sie besser anderen überlassen*. Munich: Deutscher Taschenbuch Verlag, 2014

Dörner, Dietrich. *The Logic Of Failure: Recognizing And Avoiding Error In Complex Situations*. New York: Basic Books, 1996

Dubben, Hans-Hermann, and Beck-Bornholdt, Hans-Peter. *Der Hund, der Eier legt*. Reinbek: Rowohlt Taschenbuch Verlag, 2009

Garcia, Stephen M., Tor, Avishalom, and Schiff, Tyrone M. "The Psycho- logy of Competition: A Social Comparison Perspective." *Perspectives on Psychological Science* 8(6), 2013, p. 634-650

Glass, David C., and Singer, Jerome E. *Urban stressors: Experiments on noise and social stressors*. New York: Academic Press, 1972

Gribbin, John. *In Search of Schrödinger's Cat: Quantum Physics and Reality*. New York: Bantam Books, 2013

Gumin, Heinz, and Meier, Heinrich. *Einführung in den Konstruktivismus*. Munich: Piper Verlag, 1992

Guwak, Barbara, and Strolz, Matthias. *Die vierte Kränkung: Wie wir uns in einer chaotischen Welt zurechtfinden*. Berlin: Goldegg Verlag, 2012

Hamel, Gary. *The Future of Management*. Boston: Harvard Business School Press, 2007

Harford, Tim. *Trial and Error: Warum nur Niederlagen zum Erfolg führen*. Reinbek: Rowohlt Verlag, 2012

Harris Interactive. "Obama, Jesus, and Martin Luther King Top List of America's 'Heroes'". 2009. Retrieved October 6, 2014, from http://www.harrisinteractive.com/vault/Harris-Interactive-Poll-Research-Heroes-2009-02.pdf

Hofinger, Gesine. *Fehler und Fallen beim Entscheiden in kritischen Situationen*. 2003. Retrieved August 1, 2014, from http://www.plattform-ev.de/downloads/denkfehlerhofinger.pdf

Holling, Crawford Stanley. "Understanding the Complexity of Economic, Ecological, and Social Systems." *Ecosystems* Vol. 4, 2001, p. 390-405

Holling, Crawford Stanley. "From Complex Regions to Complex Worlds." *Ecology and Society* Vol. 9 (1): 11, 2004. Retrieved August 1, 2014, from http://www.ecologyandsociety.org/vol9/iss1/art11

Holling, Crawford Stanley, Jones, Dixon D., and Peterman, R. M. "FAIL-SAFE vs. SAFE-FAIL Catastrophes." 1975. Retrieved August 27, 2014, from http://webarchive.iiasa.ac.at/Admin/PUB/Documents/WP-75-093.pdf

IBM Deutschland GmbH. "Unternehmensführung in einer komplexen Welt: Global CEO Study 2010. Retrieved August 20, 2014, from, https://www-935.ibm.com/ services/de/ceo/ceostudy2010/

IDC. "The Digital Universe of Opportunities: Rich Data and the Increasing Value of the Internet of Things." 2014. Retrieved September 28, 2014, from http://www.emc. com/collateral/analyst-reports/idc-digital-universe-2014.pdf

Janis, Irving L. *Groupthink: Psychological Studies of Policy Decisions and Fiascoes*. New York: Houghton Mifflin, 1982

Lorenz, Konrad. *Die Rückseite des Spiegels: Versuch einer Naturgeschichte menschlichen Erkennens*. Munich: Piper Verlag, 1997

Morieux, Yves, and Tollman, Peter. *Six Simple Rules: How to Manage Complexity without Getting Complicated*. Boston: Harvard Business Review Press, 2014

Mulrine, Anne. "The Army Trains a Skeptics Corps to Battle Groupthink." 2008. Retrieved October 25, 2014, from http://www.usnews.com/news/world/ articles/2008/05/15/the-army-trains-a-skeptics-corps-to-battle-groupthink?page=2

Munro, Robert. "Crowdsourcing and the crisis-affected community: Lessons learned and looking forward from Mission 4636." 2012. Retrieved October 25, 2014, from http://www.mission4636.org/report/

Pelrine, Joseph. "On Understanding Software Agility: A Social Complexity Point of View." *E:CO*, Vol. 13, Nr. 1– 2, 2011, p. 26 – 37

Pflaeging, Niels. *Organize for Complexity: How to Get Life Back Into Work to Build the High-Performance Organization*. BetaCodex Publishing, 2013

Pruckner, Maria. *Die Komplexitätsfalle: Wie sich Komplexität auf den Menschen auswirkt: vom Informationsmangel bis zum Zusammenbruch*. Norderstedt: Books on Demand GmbH, 2005

Pruckner, Maria. *Komplexität im Management. Sinn und Unsinn*. Norderstedt: Books on Demand GmbH, 2014

Richter, Klaus, and Rost, Jan-Michael. *Komplexe Systeme*. Frankfurt am Main: Fischer Taschenbuch Verlag, 2002

Rittel, Horst W. J., and Webber, Melvin M. "Dilemmas in a General Theory of Planning." *Policy Sciences* 4 (1973), p. 155 –169

Schaub, Harald. "Störungen und Fehler beim Denken und Problem- lösen." 2014, Retrieved August 1, 2014, from https://www.psychologie.uni-heidelberg.de/ ae/allg/enzykl_denken/Enz_09_Schaub.pdf

Schuh, Günther, Krumm, Stephan, and Amann, Wolfgang. *Chefsache Komplexität: Navigation für Führungskräfte*. Wiesbaden: Springer Gabler, 2013

Schulz, Kathryn. *Being Wrong: Adventures in the Margin of Error*. New York: HarperCollins, 2011

Steinmüller, Karlheinz. "Wild Cards, Schwache Signale und Web- Seismografen." Koschnick, Wolfgang J. (Ed.) *FOCUS-Jahrbuch 2012. Prognosen, Trends und Zukunftsforschung*. 2012. Retrieved September 1, 2014, from http://www. medialine.de/media/uploads/projekt/medialine/docs/ publikationen/jb_2012/ foc_jb_2012_steinmueller.pdf

Taleb, Nassim Nicholas. *Antifragile: Things That Gain from Disorder*. New York: Random House, 2012

Vester, Frederic. *Die Kunst vernetzt zu denken: Ideen und Werkzeuge für einen neuen Umgang mit Komplexität*. Munich: Deutscher Taschenbuch Verlag, 2012

von Foerster, Heinz, and Pörsken, Bernhard. *Wahrheit ist die Erfindung eines Lügners: Gespräch für Skeptiker*. Heidelberg: Carl-Auer-Systeme Verlag, 2013

von Goldammer, Eberhard. "Heterarchie – Hierarchie: Zwei komplementäre Beschreibungskategorien." *vordenker*, August 2003, http://www.vordenker.de/ heterarchy/a_heterarchie.pdf

Waldrop, M. Mitchell. *Complexity: The Emerging Science at the Edge of Order and Chaos*. New York: Simon & Schuster, 1992

Weber, Andreas. *Alles fühlt: Mensch, Natur und die Revolution der Lebenswissenschaften*. Klein Jasedow: thinkOya, 2014

Zolli, Andrew, and Healy, Ann Marie. *Resilience: Why Things Bounce Back*. New York: Simon & Schuster, 2012

About the author

Stephanie Borgert – The holistic management expert

Stephanie Borgert believes that managing can be easy, even in complex situations and turbulent times – what one needs is a holistic management approach and the right way of dealing with complexity. This is precisely the area in which Stephanie has specialized. Her passion for this topic can be sensed by those who work with her, whether in her capacity as a speaker, business consultant or management trainer. Her approach is scientifically sound and always implementation-oriented, linking knowledge from systems theory, neuroscience, and modern psychology to the management of dynamic, complex organizations.

As a business consultant

Stephanie's work is characterized by respect, openness, humor, and a solution-oriented approach. Her portfolio encompasses the following:

> *Coaching of teams in complex contexts*
> *In-house workshops for increasing organizational resilience (H.A.P.®)*
> *Impulse workshops on complexity and resilience*
> *H.A.P.® certification for coaches, consultants, executives, and project managers*

As a speaker

Stephanie's clients especially appreciate her direct, humorous style – featuring a blend of infotainment with well-grounded knowledge. Her lecture topics include:

> *Misconception 4.0 – Why digitalization is not your biggest challenge*
> *Complex is not complicated*
> *Leading in the midst of uncertainty – How to manage successfully when transparency and certainty are lacking*
> *Success "no matter what" and "come what may" – Designing resilient organizations*
> *Simple was yesterday – Projects between chaos and control*

As an author

Stephanie writes just like she works: in a clear, focused, and interdisciplinary manner, and with a twinkle in her eye. Her passion and expertise lie in the issues of complexity and resilience, which have made their presence felt in her writings from her very first book onwards.

Stephanie Borgert
Holistisches Projektmanagement
Vom Umgang mit Menschen,
Systemen und Veränderung
ISBN: 978-3-642-25701-8

Stephanie Borgert
Resilienz im Projektmanagement
Bitte anschnallen, Turbulenzen!
Erfolgskonzepte adaptiver Projekte
ISBN: 978-3-658-00999-1

Further publications by Stephanie Borgert can be found in professional journals and anthologies. An overview of these publications is available on her website, www.stephanieborgert.com.

As a person

Stephanie is a "warm and straightforward" child of the Ruhr area in western Germany. She is active with Patenmodell e.V. on a volunteer basis, helping the long-term unemployed find their way back into the working world. Stephanie finds balance in endurance sports and long walks with her two dogs. In everything that she does, she is fascinated by following new paths and discovering the unknown. She is driven by curiosity, and her work thus incorporates a highly diverse range of fields and disciplines.

GABAL global

English Editions by GABAL Publishing

Who We Are

GABAL provides proven practical knowledge and publishes media products on the topics of business, success, and life. With over 600 experienced, international authors from various industries and education, we inspire businesses and people to move forward.

GABAL. Your publisher.
Motivating. Sympathetic. Pragmatic.

These three adjectives describe the core brand of GABAL. They describe how we think, feel, and work. They describe the style and mission of our books and media. GABAL is your publisher, because we want to bring you forward. Not with finger-pointing, not divorced from reality, not pointy-headed or purely academic, but motivating in effect, sympathetic in appearance, and pragmatically-oriented toward results.

Our books have only one concern: they want to help the reader improve. In business. For success. In life.

Our target reader
People who want to develop personally and/or professionally

As a modern media house GABAL publishes books, audio books, and e-books for people and companies that want to develop further. Our books are aimed at people who are looking for knowledge about current issues in business and education that can be put into practice quickly.

For more information, see the GABAL global website:

http://www.iuniverse.com/Packages/GABAL-Global-Editions.aspx

Printed in the United States
By Bookmasters